Contents

Acknowledgements iv
List of illustrations v

Introduction 1

Part I Preparing for the journey: advice and
information to get you started 5

1 Prospects in the industry 7

2 Employment and employers 24

3 Your employability 39

4 Networking, promoting yourself and negotiation 55

5 Work experience – the key to success 66

6 Applications – first steps 79

7 Applications – next steps 97

Appendix: resources library 119

Part 2 Road to the real world: insiders' advice on
careers in the media 123

8 Film making 125

9 Television 135

10 Radio 147

11 Newspaper journalism 161

12 Magazine journalism 172

13 Publishing 183

14 Media librarianship 196

15 Multimedia 209

Index 216

Acknowledgements

The authors wish to extend their sincere thanks to all the film and media professionals who so generously gave their time and experience to help the next generation into the industry. Many thanks to Monika Kęska and Adam Wild for the photographs and Michelle Cowsley for graphics.

List of illustrations

Plates

Most media offices are hives of activity all day 9
Enjoy problem solving and getting details right 13
People work together on production projects 17
Fluent, confident communication skills are essential in
media work 22
Negotiation and teamworking skills will always be in demand 28
Setting up lighting on the set 35
Working behind the scenes can be exciting 76
Filming in progress 83
Checking equipment to get the best possible angle 91
Teamwork and concentration to get the shot exactly right 126
Andrew hard at work with his students 131
Joe Withers 133
Concentration and technical ability is important in the media 136
A typical studio at a radio station 148
Martyn Healy 153
Nicola Rees 156
Mark Poyser 158
Checking the newspapers is a daily routine for journalists 162
A great deal of time is spent in planning and preparation 174
Michaela Schoop 183
Contacting people by telephone is likely to be a
major part of the job 189
Understanding how to handle film stock is vital 198

Graphs

Radio, television and new media workforce 14
Global spending on cinema tickets, videos and DVDs 16
UK produced and/or financed films 16
Number of media studies programmes in universities 21
UK television industry workforce 137

Introduction

Welcome to *Careers in Media and Film*. We hope that you have selected this book because you want to know more about working in the film, broadcasting or media industries. If so, you have chosen wisely; this may be the book that transforms the way you think about, and manage, your career and life.

Who this book is for

If you are a student, whether you are studying film, media and related disciplines or something completely different, this book is designed to give you all the tools and information you need to become a successful manager of your own life and career. At the very least, if you follow the advice in these pages enthusiastically and conscientiously, you will gain a greater understanding of yourself, your needs and your aspirations, as well as learn how other people have planned and created careers for themselves. But we hope you will do much more than that. We believe that this book will help you to make a successful entry into the career and life that suits you, matches your personal needs and characteristics and will bring job satisfaction and happiness to you in the future, however and whatever that may mean. For graduates of any discipline, this book will give you a valuable overview of the film and media sectors and offer advice on how to you might use the skills and knowledge you have gained through your degree and apply these to finding interesting work in the media.

Perhaps you have chosen this book because you are a lecturer, teacher, academic or careers practitioner. If so, this book will enable you to support your students in their employability and personal development planning (PDP).

You will find the exercises and activities a valuable resource for supporting students to make informed decisions regarding their futures. If part of your role is teaching classes or delivering workshops, you will find the suggestions for teachers at the end of chapters offer many ideas for employability and PDP-related activities.

This book may be used as an educational text with either individuals or groups, within formal careers education courses or within advice and guidance processes.

What you will learn from this book

In this work, we have focussed particularly on careers in film and media because we have a long history and a great deal of experience of employability within this area. But much of the book explores a wide range of transferable concepts that will be useful for career development in general. Film and media continues to be a very popular area of study in both further and higher education. The subjects embrace a tremendous variety of different courses, including aspects of audio and visual media production, history and theory of film and media, with many courses offering both practical and theoretical options. Our research (Gregory, 1999) indicates that the popularity of these courses is due mainly to the fact that students believe they will help them to enter a career within the media. Popular career options include jobs in television, radio, film production or journalism. Why are they so popular? Because they are seen as dynamic, exciting and fast moving, offering fantastic opportunities for self-expression and creativity and, of course, we are all exposed to the media in all its forms all the time. For the majority of students, embarking on a course in higher education is seen as the first step towards achieving their goal: to get a great job in the media.

However, the expansion in courses has not always been met with the complete approval of employers, or the number of opportunities available. For example, Skillset (the Sector Skills Council for the Audio-Visual Industries) published a report (2003:17) showing that whilst the diverse provision of media and film education generally meets with the approval of the industries, there are concerns that students' expectations and industry's needs are not always being met. The report suggests that in order to secure employment and make an effective contribution to the sector, students need to be better equipped and have a better understanding of the skills they will need. They need better careers advice and guidance and they need to know how to enter and thrive in the working world.

This book aims to provide just that. It offers an informed view of what lies ahead if you wish to pursue a career in the media. It will also be of use to those who wish to update their careers or anyone who is considering returning to work after a career break. We will be concentrating primarily on employment in film, television, radio and journalism, but we also explore some additional careers which relate very closely to these including, for example, publishing, because we know that an open-minded, flexible approach is necessary to make the first steps into this volatile and changeable sector.

There is information on current employment trends, education, skills, work experience and typical career paths. Throughout the book there are references to real-life experiences through up-to-date case studies, providing a more personal insight into the reality of working in the media.

The authors have many years experience of teaching careers management and employability skills to students of film and media. Recently (2005) the Humanities Department at the University of Central Lancashire in Preston was designated by the government as a Centre for Excellence in the teaching of employability skills to humanities students.

This book is therefore the distilled result of many years' expertise in research, the design and delivery of careers management courses, liaising with employers and organising work experience and work placements. Our former students, who are now working as professionals within the media, feature in the case studies, where they share information about their own experiences of securing employment and progressing in their careers.

The book's approach

The book is divided into two sections. Part I is all about your career development and starts in Chapter 1 with an overview of relevant labour market intelligence, evaluating the general picture regarding employment in television, film and radio and includes data on current trends, shortages and the exciting new areas of employment which are emerging. This will be followed in Chapter 2 by an analysis of the employers' perspective, looking at the issues they identify as being of concern and passing on a wealth of insider information and advice to prospective employees. You will then be invited in Chapter 3 to identify your own employability skills, and given guidance on how to use and enhance them.

Due to the highly competitive nature of the fields of this sector, networking, making contacts and assertion skills are critical and they are covered in Chapter 4. Work experience is vitally important and in Chapter 5 you will be given some tips on maximising your chances of finding paid or unpaid work experience and guidance as to how this will improve your chances of securing the all-important first foot on the ladder. Finally, Chapters 6 and 7 will offer detailed advice on how to approach applications and interviews for employment in the media and other industries.

References within the text about websites, organisations and books can be found in detail in the resource list in the Appendix to Part I.

Part II of the book concentrates on specific areas of employment in the industry, drawing on the real experiences of people like yourselves who now work in their dream jobs. Career opportunities within these areas of work is discussed in depth and there are case studies from industry professionals, giving insights into the day-to-day challenges of the jobs and providing hints on how to get a foot on the ladder, make a personal and professional impact and ultimately progress in your chosen career.

How to get the most from this book

This work is not intended to be read passively. To be successful in employment in the 21st century you will have to take charge of your career and life. No one is going to put the effort in and do the work for you. And, like a lot of things in life, it's the effort and work you put in that will give you results. So we have created exercises, questionnaires and prompts for action that you should undertake rigorously. Like going to a gym to improve your health, these exercises will improve your career fitness. They will help you to develop a proactive approach to your own career that will have huge benefits in the years to come.

So let's not waste any more time. Let's get started with the rest of your life.

PART I

Preparing for the journey: advice and information to get you started

Welcome to Part I of *Careers in Media and Film*. Here you will find plenty of general advice and information about the opportunities available to you in this exciting sector of work. You can find out about trends in the different industries connected with media and film, learn what employers are looking for and how you can best prepare yourself for successful application. You can find out how to network and how to forge the contacts which are so vital in these professions. You will also be invited to explore the benefits and rewards of getting work experience and how to get the most out of it. This will give you lots to write about on applications and to talk about at interview, covered at the end of Part I.

ONE   Prospects in the industry

By the end of this chapter you will know more about:

- Trends in the media industries and how these relate to your career plan
- The culture and workforce in the media, film and broadcasting
- How recent graduates have successfully started careers in the media

---

This chapter explores how you might begin looking for employment within the audio-visual media industries. We look first at the pros and cons of having a qualification in a subject allied to media and whether or not this provides an advantage over degrees and diplomas in other less-closely related subject areas. This is followed by information on general trends and opportunities across the sector as well as some more specific data regarding employment in film, television and radio. The information here is by no means exhaustive so you should also research some of the industry specific literature already available. The aim here is to give you some insights into general trends across the sector. More detailed information and advice can be obtained by consulting the Appendix. In addition to facts and figures about the kinds of people who currently work in the media, the chapter presents case studies of real people, recent graduates who have stepped on to the first rung of the career ladder. They share their experience and knowledge with you and give you a few tips on how to break in at entry level.

Qualifications – have I chosen the right degree?

If you are a student on a media, communications or film studies programme, you may be concerned about your future employment prospects. Media studies in particular has suffered from a lack of recognition within traditional academic circles. This has, in turn, led to some negative press coverage of both media degrees and the subject media studies. In part, this is because the subject is relatively new and, amongst other things, it looks at aspects of popular culture such as celebrities, pop music and computer games. Critics cast doubt on the value of studying the disposable products of consumer culture and, by association, they doubt the abilities of media studies graduates. You will be glad to know is that this kind of thinking is not based on any genuine research. The good news is that the critics are ill informed.

In 2003, the Vice-Chancellor of City of London University said that 'Employment levels for media studies looked better than those for physics' (*Observer*, 17 August 2003). The research carried out on the employability of media graduates backs this up, showing very clearly, that media students are, in fact, highly employable. Indeed, they have been ranked within the top five subject areas for their employability by the Association of Graduate Careers Advisory Services (AGCAS, 2001).

This is not surprising. We live in an image-saturated world where visual literacy and an awareness of popular culture, media and film are an asset for those seeking employment in a whole range of careers. Television producers, film and advertising agency directors alike recognise that young people in particular are very knowledgeable about, and interested in, popular media. Moreover, production work is no longer confined solely to the media industries. Beyond the celebrity magazine offices and television studios in London, companies throughout the UK are making use of marketing, public relations and website activities. An up-to-date awareness of media texts and strong visual and analytical skills will also be welcome in many other enterprises. These skills are also a valuable asset to the growing number of graduates who choose self-employment at some stage in their career.

If you did not study film or media, you may have different concerns regarding your prospects of finding employment within the audio-visual industries. You may believe that you lack the very qualification which could secure you a position in television, radio, film or new media. A recent Skillset report (2004) states that only 25 per cent of those working in freelance positions within the audio-visual industries have a media degree. Employers are keen to recruit graduates from a whole range of disciplines, and specialist knowledge or enthusiasm for an unusual subject can be a tremendous asset. So, regardless of whether or not you have a media qualification, the potential for finding employment in this field is good and, if you are prepared to be flexible and find some work experience, prospects are very good indeed!

Should I go for a postgraduate qualification?

You may be considering the option of undertaking further study. If so, you need to give this very careful thought because studying at post-graduate level is very demanding and can be expensive. Begin first by questioning your motivation to continue studying. Is it because you want

Most media offices are hives of activity all day

to continue exploring a subject you love? Is it a desire to improve your chances of securing employment or to obtain an essential professional qualification? Perhaps it is a mixture of these motivations. Let's deal with these one at a time:

- **To continue studying your subject?**
  If you wish to study for another two or more years because you love the subject and can afford to do so, then go ahead. Studying a subject in depth and being free to enjoy a passion for learning are excellent experiences. There is a lot to be said for the subject knowledge and extra maturity you will be able to bring to your future career.

- **To enhance your job prospects?**
  If you believe that further study will improve your chances of securing employment, exercise a little caution. For example, you may want to become a journalist or work in public relations and this has led you to believe that an extra qualification will make you stand out from the crowd and be a more attractive proposition to an employer. Bear in mind, though, that there are employers who will take on graduates who have no postgraduate qualification. These employers would prefer to see some evidence of your potential to carry out the job and they will look at what level of skill you have to offer. They could also be interested in your potential to learn how to do the job by being trained whilst at work. Taking this into account, a postgraduate qualification may not be absolutely essential. Work experience may be a more valuable option to consider.
- **To gain professional qualifications?**
  You may believe you need a professional qualification to pursue your dream career. Take into account that it may be possible to obtain such qualifications whilst working, perhaps by part-time study or even day release. You need to investigate the options thoroughly before committing yourself and find some hard evidence to support any decision to study full time. One way of doing this would be to read advertisements for jobs in the area of work that interests you and find out whether employers do, in fact, ask for any further qualifications. If not, you might make better use of your time and save money by finding some work experience or perhaps you could spend some time as a volunteer on a project which will enable you to gain the skills you need. If the qualification is absolutely necessary, then you need to ensure that you find a college or university which has an excellent record in delivering the course you need. Ask for details of how many students have completed the qualification and where they are currently working. Try to find out what previous students have to say about the course, either by visiting and asking in person or looking at one of the unofficial guides to universities which are available on the internet (for example, www.unofficial-guides.com).

Finding information

If you do opt to take your studies further, look at all the different ways you can obtain the qualification you want. Your university library will have a copy of directories of postgraduate study such as *Hobsons* and

Prospects which have online directories of postgraduate courses (see Appendix for details). Careers libraries will be able to provide you with information about specialist or vocational courses. Also make time to visit any media careers fairs where you can ask for advice from experts. Professional organisations are another good source of information and it is well worth checking their webpages. For example, Skillset offers careers advice and information on industry-approved courses.

Financing postgrad study

Once you have made your mind up which course to take, you will have to consider how to support yourself financially (unless you are lucky enough to have rich and indulgent relatives). Some vocational courses are able to offer funding for students. A limited number of post-graduate courses attract government funding. The Arts and Humanities Research Board, for example, supports some postgraduate study in film and media. You could explore the small charities and trusts which support students by checking sources like *GrantFinder*, *Directory of Grant Making Trusts* or *Prospects Postgraduate Funding Guide*. These should be available in most good libraries. You could consider a career development loan (see www.lifelonglearning.co.uk/cdl), since these are designed to help people to overcome any financial barriers to voca-tional learning.

Keep in mind that people go into postgraduate study at many stages of their life, not necessarily straight after graduating – the door will always be open in the future.

Which industry is right for you?

Some students are certain that they would like to start a career in film, radio or television, whilst others may be less sure. You may know which industry you want to work in but have no idea about the spe-cific jobs you might be able to do. This is likely to depend on what you have studied so far and what you already know about media careers.

A good starting point is to begin your career planning by becoming more aware of general trends within the broadcasting industries since these will help you to make a better informed decision as to where to go next. Also, try to keep an open mind and look at all potential avenues. Many students limit their opportunities by refusing to look beyond a very limited range of jobs within a specific industry. Just to emphasise this point, 400 different job profiles have been identified by the sector skills council for audio-visual media (www.skillset.org.uk).

Case study: Versha

I graduated in 2003 with a Media degree and, like many students, I had no idea which career path I should follow after university. I wanted to keep my options open, which is why I chose media in the first place. It is such a broad-based subject that I felt it would give me maximum flexibility regarding career opportunities. Whilst at university, although I still was uncertain as to which area of media I should work in, I used my initiative to contact a number of newspapers and subsequently found work experience on a local evening paper.

This proved to be invaluable later on when I saw an opening for an Editorial Assistant on a national newspaper. I applied, went for an interview, and one month later I was offered the job.

At first, I found working with such experienced journalists daunting. Also some of the work can be tedious – there is a lot of administration to do. Working on a national newspaper involves high pressure, a competitive environment, and work can be pretty hectic when you are meeting deadlines but I soon got used to it. I wasn't sure what I wanted to do but this has been a great experience for me; working alongside excellent journalists and learning new skills has been invaluable. So far, I have had news-writing training, legal training and after only a year of shorthand I have reached 60 w.p.m (words per minute). I'm happy here at the moment, but in the future I would like to work in a job which involves music – maybe radio or a music magazine.

Versha's advice

If you are not sure which area of media to work in it is a good idea to get some basic experience. This way you will find out much more about different jobs which are available. On-the-job training will give you greater confidence when you do decide which area you want to specialise in. Work experience is so important – I firmly believe that my time on a local paper was one of the deciding factors when I was offered my current job. So don't worry whether it is exactly what you want to do – go out there and get as much experience as you can.

More specific information regarding popular areas of employment will be provided in Part 2. What follows next is some general information about the sector. Remember to keep in mind that there are significant areas of overlap between the different industries. For example, working as a runner on a film production is similar to the same role on a television soap. Bear in mind too that in most areas of work, employers are looking for a multi-skilled workforce.

Skills spell success

In the past, job roles were much more clearly defined and did not tend to change too much, whereas today's employee is expected to offer a

Enjoy problem solving and getting details right

wider portfolio of skills. It is also expected that you will continually update those skills and adapt them to accommodate the needs of your current employer. This is particularly the case in media production where short-term contracts and freelancing are the norm. The industry has seen an increasing emphasis on what is called 'multi-skilling', being in possession of good IT (information technology), communication, business and creative skills. 'Bi-media skilling', where camera operators may be expected to work on lighting, or presenters are asked to double up as researchers, is also more commonplace these days. Whichever area you decide to try to break into, be as proactive and strategic as you can and be prepared to learn from your efforts. This means not giving up at the first hurdle and learning to adapt your approach to finding a job where necessary. You must concentrate on maximising your skill profile, developing new skills and keeping your skills as up to date as possible.

The changing media landscape

The media landscape has changed rapidly since the 1980s when at-home entertainment took over from cinema and consumers were offered the chance to subscribe to cable or satellite television in addition to the more traditional BBC and ITV channels. Competition and choice

Radio, television and new media workforce

- Around two-thirds qualified to degree level
- Almost 66% aged 35 or under
- 61% of workforce male
- 1 in 5 have children to care for
- Disabled and minority groups under-represented
- Almost 50% of work is based in London

Radio, television and new media workforce

were emphasised within the 1990 Broadcasting Act, and this was further facilitated by the introduction of more flexible lightweight technology. With the rise of the Internet, new industries and a whole new area of entertainment have emerged around computer games and virtual realities. Advances in computer technology have also created the growing area of interactive entertainment. Spending on film, television, computer games and associated products continues to rise, leading to a wide range of employment opportunities in media production, sales and marketing. Not surprisingly, many of these jobs appeal to young graduates, particularly those with a passion for the media. Skillset estimates that there are about 400,000 people currently working in the audio-visual industry (Skillset, 2004).

Who works in the media?

You are likely to find that the majority of your colleagues will be white, male, childless graduates. The *Skillset Workforce Survey* (2004) showed that around two-thirds of those in radio, television and new media are qualified to degree level; a far higher proportion than is found in other areas of work. It also found that a similar proportion of the workforce is aged 35 or under, with only one in five having children to care for. Most of the work is located in England, with almost half the jobs based in London. The long hours and the instability of short contracts, combined with the fact that women still earn less than men, make this a less than family friendly career, which may explain why women make up only 38 per cent of the workforce. It would also be true to say that the disabled and those from black and minority ethnic backgrounds are under-represented.

However, the need for a more diverse workforce has been acknowledged by the industry. For example, the UK Film Council's (2003) plan reinforces the need to 'encourage and deliver a more diverse workforce, both culturally and socially', since this has been identified as 'being fundamental to the industry's future relevance'.

The audio-visual media industries have, in the past, been accused of nepotism, making it difficult for anyone without contacts to forge a career, but this situation is also gradually changing, with large organisations like the BBC moving towards much greater equality of opportunity within their training programmes and work-experience opportunities. This has been facilitated through the use of more rigorous recruitment strategies where diversity is promoted. So do not be discouraged if you are female, disabled, gay or from an ethnic minority.

Next we will take a closer look at the world of media production and you will be able to find out more about the current state of play within film, television and radio.

Media industry developments

Technological advances have led to a blurring of the distinctions between the different media – for instance, newspapers, television and radio programmes may now have websites. Also, more people now have access to the media and with the advent of new, lightweight technology, programmes can be made with smaller teams on lower budgets. This in turn has improved the range of opportunities available to anyone seeking a career in the media. The Universities and Colleges Admissions Service (UCAS) advertises over two and a half thousand different degree-level programmes with 'media' in the title. In 2005 there were more than five thousand graduates from media-related course. Through the growth of internet, digital, satellite and cable technology, the UK television industry now contributes £12 billion to the UK economy and a massive £440 million worldwide (UK Trade and Investment, 2005).

Although there are fewer opportunities for employment in film production than in television, the filmed entertainment industry continues to flourish. It is estimated that global spending on cinema tickets, videos and DVDs will be around £53.9 billion in 2007. Some indication of the popularity of film can be measured by the fact that there were 176 million visits to the cinema in the UK alone during 2002 (Skillset, 2002), and it is rising each year. Furthermore, UK film production activity has increased rapidly to an all-time high, creating a turnover of £1.16 billion (UK Film Council, 2003). This is reflected in the growing number of films being produced here or having UK financial involvement. The number has risen substantially, from 67 in 1993 to 134 in 2006 (www.bfi.org.uk).

All this activity has led to something of a surge in opportunities for those professionals involved in making films and in marketing and distributing them. Many students express an interest in working in film production, but it is worth bearing in mind that only 1,500 people across the UK were involved in film-making when the Skillset census was carried out.

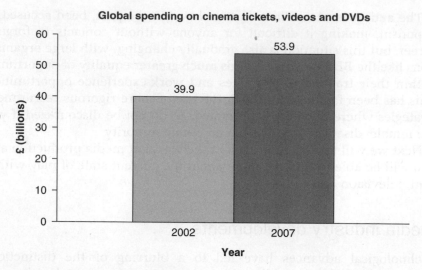

Global spending on cinema tickets

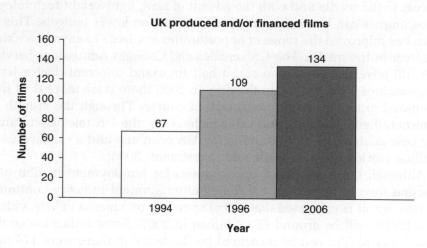

UK produced and/or financed films

Opportunities in radio

While television and film are by far the most popular areas of work for aspiring graduates, radio is often overlooked. This is a pity as it has been identified as one of the fastest growing sectors in terms of employment. There are probably more opportunities for graduates in radio than there are in television and film put together. Over the past 20 years commercial stations have increased their share of the audience to almost half of all radio listening, as shown on the industry's webpages (The Commercial Radio Companies Association www.crca.co.uk). The advent of digital

People work together on production projects

multiplex and analogue FM licences will result in an even greater increase in the number of stations, thus creating further opportunities.

The majority of students who are thinking of working in radio envisage working as either a presenter or a journalist but, depending on the size of the station, there are also many ancillary jobs in publicity and promotions or sales, finance and administration. Multi-skilling, which was mentioned earlier, is very common in radio. On the production side, it is usual for employees to come up with ideas, carry out research, present radio shows and operate equipment.

Case study: Gillian

I graduated in 2004 with upper second honours in Film and Media Studies. Before I even came to university I had done work experience with Rock FM and Magic 999 whilst at college. My initial two-week placement was extended to three, and then I arranged to go in one day a week on my day off to help out in the commercial production department because this was the area which interested me at the time. During the summer holidays I organised work experience at two other radio stations: Radio Aire in Leeds

(Continued)

(Continued)

and Century 105 in Manchester, where I was given a paid job in the sponsorship and promotions department.

I started out making cups of coffee on work experience, spending time seeing which department I liked the most. From this I started to take an interest in station branding – creating a personality for the radio station. After two years unpaid at Rock FM I decided it was time to get a paid job, so I completed my A-levels and in the summer holidays worked on the launch of Century 105 in Manchester. The job was in sponsorship and promotion and although it was office based, I saw it as a foot in the door and got my head down to work as hard as I could. Whilst working there I was offered a job at Radio Aire in Leeds. This was the turning point for me (as it is a sister station of Rock FM where I now work). The job at Radio Aire was a mixture of office and production work, so I jumped at the chance and moved to Leeds to start my new career. I stayed in the job for two years and used the time to learn everything I could about radio as a business. I also knew deep down that I would love to work in programmes as this is where I could fulfil my goal of becoming a station sound producer.

My next chance came when I was offered a job back at Rock FM as a trainee sound producer. I snapped it up and have been here for five years now. I recently achieved promotion and I am now deputy programme director. This means that I am now on a management path and one day I will programme my own radio station.

A typical day in radio could be described as madness. On the positive side, no two days are ever the same – I can be creative, and this is positively encouraged in radio. The down side is the pressure and the amount of competition out there. Being female in a male-dominated environment has been a challenge. In EMAP's Big City Network there are only two female station sound producers, and one of them is me. I am also the only female deputy programme director in the group. You have to push for what you want. There are a lot of women in the sales side of radio and they tend to do well, but programming and branding are male dominated.

Although I wouldn't say I was an 'anorak', I have always had a passion for anything radio. I grew up listening to it. It was a big part of my life. I love the fact that radio is such an instant medium. Nothing stands between you and the microphone. I enjoy creating something in my brain and then recreating the sound using voices, sound effects and music. At Rock FM I actually get involved in composing the music as well, which is extremely satisfying.

Radio is very competitive so we have to keep at the top of our game and we can't afford to make mistakes. Personally, I enjoy this challenge. I had a small break from radio in 2000 and I just couldn't keep away – it's in my blood.

Gillian's advice

Get work experience at your local radio station whether it is hospital radio, community radio or even an RSL (restricted service licence) station. Don't

(Continued)

just stick with one station, try lots and if you can get in at one station you are half way there. Once you get in, make sure you spend your time in every department to get a feel for what goes on. Find out what interests you the most – that's really important. If you are knocked back, just keep trying. Make as many contacts as possible and keep in touch with them – eventually someone will give you a break.

Working in corporate media

Finally, let's look at the corporate media sector which, even more than radio, is often overlooked by students who know little about the work that corporate professionals undertake. Sometimes referred to as the 'non-broadcast' sector, despite the fact that many companies do make use of broadcast material, this area contains a really varied range of companies, from sole traders to much larger organisations.

Typical clients range from universities, small local companies and local councils to national corporations, government, charities, multi-national corporations and institutions. These organisations make use of audio-visual media for any number of reasons: to improve business communications, for training and education purposes as well as for public relations, sales and marketing. This is a tough and competitive working environment which relies on building and maintaining excellent customer relations.

According to the International Visual Communications Association (IVCA), the UK's corporate visual communications industry has a distinguished 60-year history as well as an annual turnover of £3 billion (www.ivca.org). It may lack the glamour which attracts many to working in film or television but, for anyone seeking either essential work experience or a career in a fast moving environment, there are plenty of opportunities.

Case study: Samantha

I graduated in 2001 with a degree in Public Relations and Marketing. Before I came to university I had undertaken some work experience at a local newspaper whilst studying for my A-levels, and during my course I worked part-time in a clothing retail store. Here I had the opportunity to put my PR skills into practice helping to promote various events and gaining local press coverage.

The PR side of my degree was a balance of theoretical and practical modules. From the first year we worked on practical modules based on

(Continued)

(Continued)

real-life scenarios. This gave me a real insight into working in PR. I feel the marketing side of my degree complemented PR modules.

One of the final PR modules was to produce a portfolio of work, which included press releases, photo-calls, newsletters, articles and so on. This was an excellent tool to show at interviews, and I still keep my portfolio updated now. In my final year I was very keen to secure a job once I graduated. I started applying early and was lucky enough to be offered two PR jobs within a couple of days of each other. I ended up taking the best offer as a press officer at a local college. Since then I have worked for a creative agency and I am now currently working for University of Central Lancashire, where I have been for the past two years.

The job is very busy and extremely varied. One day I'll be writing a release about a fashion design competition, the next day I'll be creating some publicity for a new science research project. As well as creating positive publicity I also deal with potential crisis management issues. On a daily basis I liaise with the local and national press, both to create publicity and to answer any media enquiries. I produce articles for internal and external publications and the website. I have also gained basic photography skills in order to take publicity photographs to support press releases and articles, and have had my photographs published in the local press.

Samantha's advice

It is a good idea to build up a good portfolio of your work to show at interviews, and if you can gain any work experience to add to your portfolio this will help. It is important to stay focused and set yourself realistic goals.

What about the competition?

All this is very positive news for anyone wishing to find work within the media. However, whilst it is clear that within the broadcasting industries the potential for finding employment has never been better, this has to be matched against the growing number of graduates who are looking for jobs. The number of students on media studies programmes has risen from 1,200 in 1997 to over 7,000 in 2005 (Graduate Prospects, 2005). The same report shows that in 2003 there were also over 27,000 graduates from arts, creative arts and humanities courses. Since the majority of graduate vacancies are open to graduates of any discipline, you will find that the competition for jobs can be fierce. This is particularly the case in the very popular areas – film, television and radio production, where graduates can find themselves working for little or nothing in order to get a foot in the door.

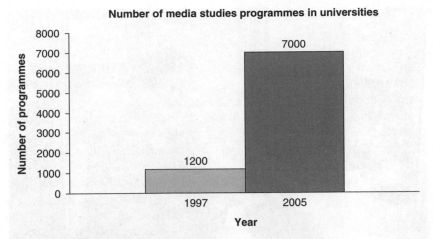

Number of UK media studies programmes in universities

According to Jenkins (2003, p.10) 'It's estimated that 60,000 people try to break into the audio-visual industries in the UK television, radio, film and interactive media industries, every year. That's a lot, considering 200,000 already work in them.' Although job-seekers will find that this is a highly competitive sector, they may be surprised to find that a number of skills shortages have been identified. In television there is a shortage of script editors, accountants and rights managers; furthermore, accountants in film production and animation are in short supply. Scriptwriters, producers, storyboarders and editors are also needed in animation (Skillset, 2004). The message here is that it is worth taking the time to investigate areas of skills shortage as well as the more popular careers if you wish to maximise your chances of obtaining work. It can also be productive to consider the value of additional training which may enable you to take on one of these roles.

Is a degree necessary?

Despite the competitive nature of the industry, you may also be surprised to find that a degree is not always seen as a necessary requirement for employment. Many people in the sector worked their way up by starting at the bottom and being trained on the job. This means that you may find yourself working alongside non-graduates. But remember, your degree or diploma is still a very valuable addition to your career's portfolio and it provides you with an added bonus if you decide to change jobs later on. If, for example, you decide further

Fluent, confident communication skills are essential in media work

along the line that you would like to move from media production to teaching media studies, your degree will be an essential qualification. Graduates with a degree in media or film are also able to find employment in a whole range of careers, from teaching, librarianship and arts management to heritage, exhibition, museum and gallery work.

It is important not to give up at the first hurdle. It may be difficult to break into the media but if you have determination and drive, and are prepared to make use of the advice and information offered within the following chapters, you can create the career of your dreams. A degree or diploma in film and media or humanities may not guarantee that you get your dream job but one thing is certain: you will have acquired valuable skills and knowledge during your years of study. This will give you an advantage in starting your career, especially if you are willing to gain some all-important work experience to add to your personal portfolio of skills, knowledge and talents. Most degree level programmes enable you to develop a range of generic, transferable skills alongside the more specific subject knowledge. Examples of these skills include time management and self-management, teamworking, leadership, oral and written communication skills. You will also be able to offer research, presentation and IT skills, since the majority of degree programmes will have encouraged you to develop them.

Some students will have been fortunate enough to have undertaken work placements within their course, as most universities now actively engage in promoting employability skills. It is also a fact that the majority of students are engaged in some part-time employment or voluntary work whilst at university, and this work experience can also help if you are able to relate it to the job you want. It is important to remember that all work experience can add value. Work experience will be dealt with in more depth in Chapter 5, but for the time being you need to keep in mind that, with greater awareness, you can rise to the challenge of competition by integrating your whole life experience into your job seeking-strategy.

Notes for teachers

This chapter offers a thorough overview of the culture, history and trends within the film and media industries and introduces readers to some real-life case studies of graduates who have successfully entered the field. This is intended to give students an informed starting point for how they might approach their own career strategy. In the classroom this can be enhanced by activities such as:

- In teams or individually, students take one career field, for example, radio, then research in detail the range of jobs within it.
- Students present their research to each other perhaps in the form of an exhibition, poster display, talks or booklets.
- National and local destination information can be probed to reveal statistical and other evidence of graduate employment within media careers.
- Students can take responsibility to contact recent graduates in the field to ask them to act as visiting speakers.

TWO   Employment and employers

By the end of this chapter you will know more about:

- The current employment situation within film and media industries
- Which skills are most in demand in the film and media industries
- How employers started and built their media businesses and careers

---

Setting the scene

Having explored the nature of the sector and the prospects for work when you graduate, this chapter will help you to look at work from the employers' perspective. You will find out how the sector has evolved and changed and the impact of these changes on the career you may pursue. This wider context will enable you to appreciate why employers are looking for certain skills and attributes and why they are sometimes frustrated in their search for suitable employees. You will also find some quotes from employers, explaining what they want from you. By increasing your awareness, the information in this chapter will enable you to discover the best ways to make an impact when you approach employers and help you to avoid some of the potential pitfalls. With all this in mind, you can then take an audit of your own relevant employability skills, identify where you could improve any weaknesses, and so become more employable in the industry.

The changing nature of the sector

The audio-visual industries have gone through a period of very radical change over the past two decades. It was noted in the previous chapter that freelance working is a key factor, particularly in the area of media production. These high levels of self-employment reflect changes which began during the 1980s when new labour laws were introduced and the power of trade unions was curtailed. In broadcasting, for example, before the 1980s, entry into the limited number of large media organisations was carefully controlled and permanent staff jobs were much more common. The big corporations also carried out their own training programmes and career progression was quite clearly structured. Employers in the newer and smaller post-1980s independent companies prefer to engage staff on a flexible basis. The vast majority of companies now offering employment are small-to medium-sized enterprises, employing an average of only about 20 people. Many of these employees are working on short-term contracts and job security is limited. Some indication of the current state of play can be gathered from a recent census which revealed that the numbers working freelance in the audio-visual industries range from 98 per cent in film production to 35 per cent in broadcast radio. The lowest levels of self-employment have been found in cinema exhibition, cable and satellite television (Skillset, 2004). In the closely allied creative and cultural industries sector, which encompasses music and performing arts, crafts, advertising, heritage, visual and literary arts, the situation is broadly similar.

Although this sector contributes substantially towards the economy, with consumer spending on music alone accounting for over £4 billion, the majority of businesses are small, with many having less than 10 employees on the payroll. Part-time working patterns are common, with one-quarter of employees working less than 30 hours a week (AGCAS Sector Briefings: Cultural Sector, 2005). Like the audio-visual industries, this is a sector which attracts a high proportion of graduates. Career progression is loosely structured and employees are encouraged to augment their creativity with a portfolio of additional skills, incorporating everything from fund-raising and business awareness to an understanding of health and safety regulations.

Graduates, having invested much time, effort and money in studying for a degree to improve their career prospects, are often understandably disheartened at the prospect of short-term contracts and limited job security. They are also concerned by the additional pressure of being expected to undergo frequent training in order to stay in employment.

However, it is important to keep this in perspective. The world of graduate employment has changed radically in recent times and the fact is that in many areas of work 'jobs for life' are non-existent. Employers in most sectors expect staff to update their skills regularly and to offer flexibility. Young people leaving college or university today, regardless of which career they enter, can expect to change their job several times throughout their working life. Indeed, many may also change their career more than once. It is best to view these challenges in a positive light. Look at your career as an interesting journey with many destinations and prepare yourself for the adventure which lies ahead.

So what do employers want?

Unless you intend to try self-employment as soon as you graduate, you will be working for someone else. In order to be successful, you need to look at things from their point of view from the outset. It might seem somewhat obvious to tell you that employers are looking to fill vacancies with talented and skilled people, but this is essentially the case! Enthusiasm alone is not enough. However keen you might be to get into the media, whether as a presenter, writer, researcher, marketer or sales professional, you are unlikely to get a job unless you have the all-important prerequisite skills and capabilities. Not only do you need to be in possession of the right skills, you also need to be able to demonstrate your ability to someone who is busy and has other candidates to consider. Look at this from the employer's perspective. Taking on a new employee involves taking a risk. Your employer will have to invest time, money and trust in any new recruits. Would you be prepared to take a risk and employ someone who is unable to show you that they can do the job?

Graduates naturally tend to value their education and the qualifications that they have so recently worked hard to acquire. Conversely, they undervalue, or find it hard to understand, the importance of the skills which they possess. This is not surprising when, for the past few years, exams and grades have virtually taken over your life. You need to take on board that employers generally value your skills much more highly than you do. Furthermore, they like to see a range of generic skills in addition to the more specialised-job specific skills. These skills may be called a lot of different names:

- Key skills
- Competencies
- Soft skills
- Transferable skills
- Employability skills

According to the Higher Education Careers Service Unit (HECSU), the skills most popular with graduate recruiters include:

- **communication** – the ability to communicate fluently, whether this be verbal, in writing or via electronic means;
- **teamwork** – being a useful team player, contributing positively to the success of a group;
- **leadership** – being able to support, motivate and encourage others, as well as take the lead when appropriate;
- **initiative** – the ability independently to see opportunities and achieve tasks;

- **creative problem solving** – thinking things through in a creative, structured and imaginative manner in order to work out issues;
- **flexibility/adaptability** – ability to handle change positively, respond to setbacks and adapt to new situations;
- **self-awareness** – knowing your strengths, weaknesses, motivations, goals and skills, and being able to explain and describe these to others;
- **commitment/motivation** – having energy and enthusiasm in work, learning and life;
- **interpersonal skills** – the ability to get on well with others and to establish sound working relationships;
- **numeracy** – competence and understanding of basic numbers in practical contexts such as business.

Let's look at each of these in more detail.

Communication skills

Speaking clearly, writing well and listening carefully are important in all areas of work. This is particularly true in business, where poor communication can hinder profitability. In the creative sector, where small businesses dominate, the ability to sell ideas is absolutely fundamental to survival. Employers are looking for people who can explain concepts and enthuse or persuade others. Listening skills and the ability to interpret ideas orally and in writing are essential for effective business communication.

Make sure that any contact you make with an employer, by phone, email or letter, showcases your communication skills. A mumbled phone message or badly written letter will not do you any favours. Use the interview to demonstrate your ability to communicate (interview technique will be covered in detail in Chapter 7).

If you are looking for sales or marketing roles, the same approach applies. Think of an example of how you have been able to influence and persuade others, whether in paid or voluntary employment or at university if you have been involved in any associations or activities.

Teamwork

At last you can see the point of all those group projects and how useful it is to have worked in a bar, shop or restaurant. Everyone in the media needs to be able to work effectively, enthusiastically and courteously with other people. Prima donnas and shrinking violets will not be tolerated. Your team will be depending on you, however humble your

Negotiation and teamworking skills will always be in demand

role, so fundamentals like being on time, greeting people politely, offering a helping hand, making yourself useful at all times and just getting on happily with others are absolutely critical. If you don't feel you can do this, then you won't fit into the industry.

Leadership

This sounds like the exact opposite of teamwork and in some ways it is, but employers do want everything. As well as getting on with others they want you to be able to take responsibility, complete set tasks with little or no supervision and even support other people. This is a lot to ask, especially of a new graduate, but if you display that you have the potential to lead it will impress most employers.

Initiative

Have you done nothing but sit at a computer screen and attend the odd class for the last three or four years? If so, you will not impress a potential employer – definitely not in the creative or media industries. You must show that you have done interesting things above and beyond the minimal everyday student-type activities. If you want to break into the film, media, broadcasting or any other creative industry, you must demonstrate that you have been involved in some relevant activity, whether this is writing for a fan magazine or creating a blog, doing some amateur dramatics, playing in a band – anything that shows your initiative. If you haven't done anything much as yet, do something now.

Creative problem solving

A common complaint is that graduates are simply not creative enough, and employers are anxious to find individuals who can demonstrate proven creative ability or outstanding creative potential. These qualities are valued so highly by employers because the audio-visual and cultural industries rely heavily on imagination and vision. From an employer's perspective, the ability to come up with new ideas and find novel solutions to problems can generate income, therefore raw recruits who can demonstrate these capabilities are much more likely to succeed. Examples of creativity do not have to be highly artistic: a successful candidate who invented a better way of managing the staff rota at the night club where she worked was showing a creative approach to her job, which she could then talk about at interview.

Case study: an employer's view

Richard Scott of Axis Animation said that highly creative people are thin on the ground. Regrettably, he sometimes has to resort to employing graduates from outside the UK to fill a creative skills gap within his company (Skillset Careers Event, 'Careering in the Audio Visual Industries', Tuesday 21 March 2006, The Commonwealth Club, London). You might believe that the fact that you have studied film production, animation or creative writing provides sufficient evidence of your creativity, but from an employer's perspective you must be able to offer plenty of examples of your ability to generate ideas, to interpret them in writing or as a media artefact.

One way of providing evidence of your talent is by showing an example of your work. If you want to work in film production, demonstrate that you have originality by showing a film you have made. Budding presenters need to provide evidence of their ability with a well thought out showreel. For those of you who would like to write for a living, you need to produce a portfolio of work which shows versatility and originality. Whilst at university or college, try to find plenty of creative work experience – on the university radio station, in a theatre group or arts organisation. Not only will this give you greater confidence, it will provide you with the raw materials to show off your creative potential.

Flexibility/adaptability

Clearly, the needs of employers differ depending on which area of the media and culture industries you wish to break into, but there are some common requirements. For instance, the majority of employers in all companies are looking to recruit people who are flexible in their approach to work and prepared to undertake more than one role if and when necessary. This need for flexibility is currently very acute in the interactive media industry.

Employer comment

Ian Morrison, Chairman of Carlyle Media and Chair of the Interactive Media Skills Group, said: 'The sector depends on high-end skills, but since it is largely made up of small businesses, there is a reliance on multi-tasking to cope with the new skills needed to keep pace with the speed at which technology advances' (www.skillset.org/skillset/press/2004/article_2980_1.asp).

In the most popular areas of employment, where there are more graduates looking for work than there are jobs for them, employers can afford to be extremely choosy. This is particularly noticeable in the film industry. At a Skillset careers event (2006), Marc Samuelson, head of Samuelson Productions, said that as there are only around 1,000 jobs available annually in film and with 18,000 graduates applying for them, it is not surprising that competition is fierce. He also pointed out that, regrettably, in some cases this has led to exploitation, particularly at the junior end where long hours and bad pay are a reality for many young people. Like a lot of employers, he stressed the fundamental importance of talent and good skills.

Self-awareness

The fact that you are reading this book suggests that you are someone with raised awareness. You probably have ideas about who you are, what your passions, qualifications and skills are, and where you might want to use these in the future. This makes you self-aware. The trick now is to clarify and communicate your self-knowledge so that someone else (an employer or a client) can recognise you and value what you have to offer. All through our life we can develop increasing self-awareness and find better and better ways to express this to others. Probably one of the attractions of working in the creative and cultural fields is that you get to express your inner thoughts to other people. It is therefore even more important in this sector that you can explain yourself to others. Completing the exercises suggested in this book will greatly help you in this process.

Commitment/motivation

Attitude is seen as all-important, and this is measured by the applicant's determination to succeed, to work hard and to give 101 per cent. These qualities are difficult to assess in an interview, but at least you have a chance to give examples of times when you have put in extra effort, on work experience whilst at university or within extra-curricular activities. You might have managed to combine full-time study with a part-time job where you have been given promotion. Perhaps you have been manager of the university football team, or you could have been involved in a challenging volunteering project. If you want to stand out at interview, be ready to show that you are a person who is willing to go that extra mile.

Motivation and enthusiasm are essential qualities in the eyes of employers. It might seem obvious that if you want to work in television, you need to watch programmes and be able to talk about your viewing. However, employers have cited examples of graduates coming to interviews unable or unwilling to talk about the medium. So, while you may be thinking that the very fact that you have chosen to study media at university indicates your enthusiasm for the subject, you still need to convey this enthusiasm. Make sure that you have an in-depth knowledge of something which excites you and be willing to talk about it with some passion.

Interpersonal skills

The likeability factor is a strong indicator of future success for many employers. Since working in the media often involves working closely in small teams, you need to show that you are easy to get along with, which means to an employer that you will probably work well in a team. Also included is care and consideration of others' points of view, ability to listen as well as contribute to discussions, meetings and in one-to-one dialogue, body language, appearance and general social skills.

Numeracy

Don't worry if you are unable to solve simultaneous equations. When employers talk about numeracy, what they often are referring to is awareness of how business works and an understanding of the importance of making or saving money wherever possible.

Employer comment
Head of Client Services and Graduate Recruitment at one of the world's largest advertising agencies, Ian Pearman says that the work is

'not just about creating fantastic advertisements but that it is a business, creating revenue and profits'. He also highlights the importance of interpersonal skills in an effective business. Since the majority of employers in this field are small-scale enterprises, this is a crucial factor in maintaining a competitive edge. Whilst you may argue that you chose to study media or film, not accountancy, working in a small business will inevitably mean that you will need to gain some business sense rapidly. There are some suggestions of how you might do this in the table later in this chapter.

Employer case studies

As we have said, the majority of audio-visual media companies are small- or medium-sized businesses, some run by only one or two people. The case studies which follow are included to give you an insight into the nature of two typical companies.

Case study: ADI

ADI is an outside broadcasting and post-production company typical of the small- to medium-size enterprises which dominate the UK audio-visual industries. It was established in 1991 and over the years has developed several disciplines including outside broadcast, programming and post-production facilities. The company currently employs approximately 45 full-time staff and uses a wide variety of freelance crew to fulfil contracts. They work with a number of premiership football clubs – including Manchester United FC and Liverpool FC filming programmes that are televised on MU TV's Channel and the international market for LFC TV. The post-production department has produced DVD/videos for Bentley cars, councils and the emergency services for educational purposes or for induction, and health and safety DVDs/videos.

Staff roles and responsibilities

Staff are recruited to a number of roles within the company. Examples include:

- *Broadcast Engineer* – The engineers prepare the outside broadcast vehicles (OBs) at base to the specification of each job we receive, and then will go and rig at the site of the event and guarantee the OB during the event and then de-rig afterwards with the team booked on the job, which will include camera/sound/vision operators and riggers/drivers.

(Continued)

(Continued)

- *Editor* – The editors are provided with a brief from the client and will edit adverts and football match programmes for match days. The client does not always know what they want, therefore the editor will offer creative advice and may even produce something without a spec. for the client to see before deciding on the final edit.

Recruitment

Various approaches are used to recruit staff and this is generally dependent on the position to be filled.

- *Administrative/office roles* – local newspapers, recruitment agencies or recommendations.
- *Technical/production roles* – *Broadcast* magazine, recommendations, universities, specialist recruitment agencies.

Work experience

ADI does offer work experience, the length of which can vary dependent upon the project. Work experience is unpaid but travel expenses are reimbursed. Work experience can lead to freelance work, and students have been offered full-time work after a period of working freelance or on a placement.

Advice from ADI

Even though this is a difficult industry to break into it is achievable, so be persistent. People who make the effort stand out from the rest. We hate to receive badly composed cover letters with spelling errors and bad punctuation. Some students have taken the time to research the company but there are a few who don't take the trouble despite the fact that the company has an easily accessible website. We expect any interested student to have looked at our website in some detail.

Case study: Dragon's Garden

Dragon's Garden is a small enterprise, established in 2003 by director John McBride. John had always been a huge movie fan and had studied related subjects at both college and university. When he started work he took office jobs and developed his career studying accountancy whilst

(Continued)

(Continued)

working as an accounts manager for a small firm. Meanwhile he also worked on a few photography projects such as staff photos for reception displays and photographing events.

In the back of his mind he always wanted to work on films, so eventually he decided to start his own production company. He taught himself how to set it up, how to do tax returns and found out about insurance-related law. Fortunately he had an accounts background and was able to do his own. Next he started to work on some small projects filming for charities and working with youth groups. Over the first year he used all his holiday entitlement to work on the business, sourcing new business funding and working at evenings and weekends to build up a small client base. After a year he left his accounts job to work on the business full time.

John is the only full-time employee in the business, although he does rely on the services of a commercial manager to deal with contracts and to liaise with clients. He is a member of BECTU (media trade union), which offers support if he needs legal representation. John also produces and directs short films and documentaries.

We asked John for some detailed information about his career and company.

- **How do you find work as a freelancer?**
  'My core client base is local education authorities, charities and a few organisations who come to me when they need training videos. I have worked for Cancer Research, the British Anti Vivisection Association, Lancashire Education Authority, Drugline, Heritage Lottery, the Liberal Democrats and many others. These corporate jobs pay the bills! Another good source of income is to freelance for other firms. They hire me as a second cameraman or a production manager. Those jobs are easy because I just do that single job and I don't have the added worries of keeping my clients happy and working to strict budgets and deadlines. I worked on a feature film in 2004 for six months, line producing it and was the production manager on it as well.'
- **Do you employ anyone else?**
  I employ freelancers as and when they are needed, depending on the project. I might only employ one person to work with me for a few days or I might employ several over a course of a few months. I don't employ anyone full time. It's not something I want to rush into.'

Setting up lighting on the set

- **Could you describe some of the roles undertaken by staff?**
  'Because my business is small, I am usually on the look-out for an assistant who could get their teeth into a few things. It would probably be just the two of us, so I'd need someone to work the phones, set up lights, help move equipment, swinging the boom or operating lights, that sort of thing. On larger productions there could be many people working voluntarily. For instance, I made a film called *Green Shoes* last year. The story revolved around a group of people on a night out and how one of the female characters was attacked and raped. We got some funding from the UK

Film Council, but £1,000 doesn't go very far! I needed two leads, four main characters, 12 minor characters plus around ten extras. We needed a crew (DoP, first and second ADs, production assistants, make-up girls and so on), so in the end we had 55 people working on a 10-minute short with that £1,000 budget. The budget just about covered the food, drink and expenses, but everyone gave up their time and skills to work for free. When you are doing this sort of stuff it becomes second nature to negotiate the right deals with people and you learn how to do things with no money. Then you can make whatever films you like.'

- **How do you recruit staff?**
'I post ads with *Shooting People* and *Talent Circle* for specific jobs. I'll contact agencies for staff and actors as well. Sometimes I approach colleges and universities, and I will discuss projects in newspapers and magazines during interviews that attract attention. A lot of the time I approach people I have worked with in the past and either employ them or ask them if they know someone who can help me.'

- **Do you offer work experience? If so, for how long and is it paid or unpaid?**
'Yes, I've offered work placements. I was paid to train a couple of lads with my camera and sound equipment for the film *Chicken Tikka Masala* and we made the 'behind the scenes' documentary. I paid the lads £500 each and found them accommodation for a month.

'I've also had someone with me over the summer working on all different aspects of the business from accounting, to recruiting right through to filming and editing. He was paid £200 a week by the local council through a special arts-based business training scheme. There are little pots of money available for individuals like that, but more often than not these pots of money will be for groups and societies, so it could be that I could tap into some money through a charity or local authority and spend a few weeks teaching new skills to youth groups or ethnic groups.

'Come to think of it, I suppose with the way the shorts get made with the people involved giving their time for free, there is an element of training there anyway and those giving up their time know they will be taking something away from the project.'

- **Do you experience any problems recruiting staff?**
'I have had people not show up for interviews, and that really annoys me. I don't like giving up my time for people simply not

to bother. I don't like people sending speculative CVs. I simply don't have the time to read them. One thing people have to know is that it's not a nine-to-five job. I can start at 5 a.m. and finish at midnight (yes, a 19-hour day), or work six nights in a row 6 till 6. People have to be ready to give their energy to work like that, and a lot aren't ready for it. When I worked on *Chicken Tikka Masala* I worked about 13–16 hours per day, six days a week for six months, and at the end I was physically exhausted.

'People can also screw up shots by not paying attention and when you are on tight deadlines it's important to know exactly what is going on, so concentration is a must. Working on films can be boring sometimes, but the crew needs to be ready to jump into action. Do I sound like an ogre? I'm quite nice really!'

- **What advice would you give to young people who are keen to work in the media?**
'Work at it. Keep going and work on as much stuff as you can. Be ready to work for free. You'll find people start paying you once they know you can do it. One thing leads to another.

'Above all, push yourself. If you make your own stuff be ready for loads of negative reviews and feedback, but learn from it and keep going. Erm … and have fun doing it too!

'Now you know a little more about the concerns and everyday practises of typical companies you might find yourself working for, it's time to think about the value of your degree or diploma within the workplace.'

- **How to use your qualifications to maximise your chances of success?**
'Students and graduates are often surprised to hear that approxi-mately 60 per cent of all graduate vacancies do not specify a degree subject.

'Two-thirds (67.6 per cent) of the vacancies on offer in the 2005/6 issue of *Prospects Directory* are open to graduates from any disci-pline, reflecting the trend that many employers are looking for the 'soft' skills that graduates acquired during their study rather than their knowledge in a specific subject (Prospect Directory Salary and Vacancy Survey 05/06).

'So the subject and class of your degree are often less important to the employer than what you can actually do. This means that whether you have a degree in history, music or film studies, employ-ers acknowledge that you are likely to be in possession of a range of analytical, research, organisational and communication skills.

'There are, of course, some specialist areas where specific qualifications are needed and skills shortages in certain industries can create very particular demands. This is currently the case in the audio-visual industries where a skills gap has led to a demand for business graduates to fill sales, marketing, administrative, accounting and financial planning roles (Jenkins, 2003: 10). This means that graduates are going to have to look very closely at their skills and try increasingly to meet the needs of potential employers.'

The next chapter will help you to look at your employability and make the most of your skills and talents.

Notes for teachers

This chapter introduces the important concept of employability. In any class some students will be interested in entering the industry but others will not – the main point is that whatever they wish to do, their employability is important and something they will work on all their life.

- Involve employers – small groups interview a local employer (not necessarily in the media) to discover what skills they want from their employees.
- Students may research employment experiences by interviewing family members or friends (primary research) or by library activities.
- They can then discuss how employability has changed over the years and predict the trends of the future.
- Class members can find examples of employability skills in vacancies or from direct experiences in work.
- Pairs or small groups make a poster showing a person with employability – what would they look like? What would they do?

THREE   Your employability

By the end of this chapter you will know more about:

- What employability means
- Your own employability skills and how to record them
- How to enhance your employability for the film and media industries

Employability – the key to your career

How can you get into work in the film and media industries? There is such a great diversity of jobs, occupations, vocations and careers to be found and enjoyed in this broad field. Media people may be runners in television studios or online journalists, film directors or radio announcers, music critics or acting coaches or many other roles. Perhaps you think all these people can't have any one thing in common – but they can. They possess employability. They have secured their job and are managing to keep it and be successful at it because they have the right mix of skills, aptitudes, knowledge and experience. They are employable. Understanding what makes them employable can show you the way to becoming successful in the world of media.

Once you know how to improve and build upon your own employability you will be in a far better position to apply for, and successfully enter, your chosen field in media. And incidentally, should you change your mind about working in film and media, you will be able to transfer to other careers or professions more easily.

So what is this (almost) magical ingredient, and how are you going to get it?

What is employability?

First, let's look at what employability isn't: it isn't just getting a job; it isn't just being in a job.

Employability is about being able to find what you really want in life. It is about balancing your life so there is time and room for what you want. It is about understanding what motivates you and turns you on. It is about taking control of the exciting adventure that is your future. Employability enables you to reach your own personal and working fulfilment. It gives you the power to make decisions for yourself that are based on reality, not fantasy. It helps you to make the most of the opportunities around you, but more importantly to create new and relevant opportunities for yourself. Possessing employability gives you increased security in an increasingly insecure world. Of all the people employed in media, for example, 40 per cent are self-employed and a further 10 per cent work at some time on a freelance basis, so you can see that managing your own career path is a vital skill for success in the media.

Graduate's tip

Simon Brisk now works at Mersey TV but he spent several years on short contracts working for Granada TV. He advises: 'Be prepared to work on short contracts and in temporary jobs to get that vital experience. Never turn down the offer of a bit of work – it can lead to better things.'

Auditing your employability – step 1

What makes you an employable individual? You might think it's your qualifications or previous experience or some special technical skills that you have. In fact, although these things are important and valuable, they do not on their own make you employable.

Look carefully at these adverts for jobs within the world of media and film. Do you notice how many times personality characteristics and qualities are mentioned? Employers, particularly in the creative fields, are often looking for qualities such as team skills, determination, creativity, enthusiasm, and the ability to work effectively with others or on your own initiative.

Exciting opportunity for a Creative Director to join a small B2B marketing communications company with a great client base. In this client-facing role, you will have a practical approach

(Continued)

to project/people management with a strong commercial awareness and lots of drive as you will be leading/advising a team of designers from concept to delivery of a variety of mainly BTL print projects. Good conceptual, organisational and people management skills are a prerequisite coupled with a creative mind and strong hands-on Mac skills. Basic Dreamweaver and Flash would be a bonus. Please send CV and samples to marcus@workshystation.co.uk. We apologise but we are only able to respond to successful applicants.

We are looking for a talented, dynamic, enthusiastic and creative Producer/Director to join a VT team. Applicants must have proven experience of shooting short VTs and be able to make films on a variety of subjects, from cookery to comedy and everything in between, often on a tight schedule. Please include your last TV credit and current rate along with your CV.

Award-winning DM agency seeks a meticulous proactive Production Manager to oversee all aspects of production in their busy studio. Main responsibilities will be to: build and maintain excellent relationships with clients, suppliers and internal departments; manage artwork production through internal studio and art buying when necessary; and ensure that procedures and systems are adhered to. Candidates must have good communication and organisational skills, at least three years' previous production experience in a below-the-line agency, and be able to traffic, budget and problem solve to a very high standard. We are sorry but we can only reply to shortlisted applicants.

Have you got an exciting way with words?
COPYWRITER
If the answer's a very convincing 'yes', then here's your chance to put your creative writing skills to the test in a fast-moving commercial environment working for Please Wait UK.

(Continued)

(Continued)

As the country's leading provider of on-hold marketing, we've built a powerful reputation for creating on-hold marketing productions that stand out from all the rest, which is why we now need yet more creative writing talent to help us maintain our very high standards – standards which have won us clients as prestigious as Coca Cola, P&O Ferries, Audi UK and Sport England.

As part of our in-house creative team you'll be working alongside account managers and sound producers, helping to write fresh and invigorating marketing material for our clients to play to their telephone callers when they place them on hold. No two clients are the same, which is why you'll need a fearless approach to writing about companies large and small, stacks of original ideas and the ability to balance creative thinking with the demands of a business-focused media environment.

Sounds like you? Then send your CV to me, Daye Wilson, at the following email address: hrmanager@pleasehold.co.uk.

Reading job descriptions, personnel specifications and vacancies will soon reveal how important employability skills are in the minds of employers. They want people who possess these personal and interpersonal aptitudes and characteristics, and the more of these you can develop, the more employable you will be.

TIP

Start now to collect vacancies in the careers that interest you. Don't worry if you couldn't possibly apply for the jobs. The purpose is to learn what the employers are looking for. If you want to, send for the further information and application form, or study the online form if you can get access. Keep the vacancies in your job file.

Auditing your employability – step 2

People are often far more employable than they first realise. It is quite difficult to assess how employable you really are unless you spend a bit of time thinking about your past experiences. Most of us just don't do this, unless we have to do an exercise like this one.

This list of skills, qualities and useful aptitudes is based on the ones most in demand from an employer's point of view, as outlined in the previous chapter. For each of them, try to find an example of where you might have developed or used this skill. Don't worry about whether it was at home, in sport, part-time or temporary work, voluntary work, community or family activities, college, school or university or anywhere else. Just concentrate on yourself and what you have experienced. Make your examples as clear and concrete as possible. If you get stuck, there are little examples to prompt you. It can also help to rate yourself out of ten for each of the skills so you can identify any strengths or weak areas. Write your example(s) in the last column.

TIP

This list also makes an excellent starting point for redeveloping your CV or writing an application form.

Most people do find they have a good range of employability skills which they can identify from previous experiences. If you have identified a lot of good examples, that is great. Your only task now will be to keep improving these skills and expanding your skills base still further. You will learn how to make the most of these skills for applications and interviews later.

TIP

Make a special note of any job or employer that particularly appeals to you, even though you might not be able to apply for the job now. They might be ones you can apply for in the future.

COMMUNICATION/ INTERPERSONAL SKILLS	A specific example (or examples) where you have exercised this skill
Relating to customers, clients or the public; in person and/or by telephone.	
Making a verbal presentation to people: • who you know and are familiar with; • who are new to you, for instance, in an interview or selection process.	
Using verbal skills to persuade, negotiate, confer, arrange and agree some activity or event with others.	
Composing and writing correct formal business documents; e.g. letters, emails, memos, faxes.	
Creating and writing effectively business reports, agenda, minutes and so on.	
Researching a set topic or subject; finding your own sources of written information.	
Writing creatively for a specific purpose, e.g., script-writing, screen-writing, short stories, novels.	
Using visual media to express ideas or concepts.	
Prompts: think about presentations for college or uni; work with the general public in part-time jobs; reports or articles for different subjects; and using the telephone for formal purposes.	

TEAMWORKING, LEADERSHIP AND INITIATIVE	A specific example (or examples) where you have exercised this skill
Cooperating with others in a group to complete a time-bound project (for example, short film, exhibition, published work).	
Planning and agreeing with others: • group or team objectives; • responsibilities and working arrangements within a group or team.	
Organising your own activities so that you can be effective and efficient in a group or team.	
Dealing with any difficulties in group or team activities.	
Leading a group in a specific task or activity.	
Taking the initiative to change, adapt or improve something.	

Prompts: any kind of team activities will be of interest, including sporting teams, charity team events, working with others on projects or group work and, of course, any part-time jobs nearly always involve teamwork.

CREATIVITY AND SOLVING PROBLEMS	A specific example (or examples) where you have exercised this skill
Identifying the main features of a problem you need to solve and deciding how to solve it.	
Reviewing your problem-solving techniques and improving skills.	
Identifying independently something new that needs to be done.	
Thinking independently to find creative solutions to problems.	

Prompts: think about any challenge you have overcome (as long as it is not too delicate), issues of work–life–study balance, adjusting to new situations, family problems, travel or hobbies.

FLEXIBILITY/ ADAPTABILITY	A specific example (or examples) where you have exercised this skill
Coping effectively with a major change in your life, work or study.	
Being adaptable, able to change.	

Prompts: examples might include adapting to sixth form or college, becoming a mature student, a change of role at work, going to university.

SELF-AWARENESS	A specific example (or examples) where you have developed this aptitude
Being aware of your own skills, interests, values, motivations and goals.	
Explain what methods of learning and working suit you best.	
Identify what makes you unique and what you can offer.	
Able to describe yourself appropriately to others.	

Prompts: any interview or selection process you have undertaken, completing a record of achievement or personal portfolio, writing about your experiences on a weblog, all could be useful.

COMMITMENT/ MOTIVATION	A specific example (or examples) where you have displayed this attitude
Carrying something through and showing determination.	
Showing high levels of motivation towards a goal.	
Being enthusiastic.	
Prompts: this is asking for examples of where you have successfully completed something such as an award, sporting activity, arranging an event or holiday, even completing a college course under difficult circumstances.	

NUMERACY SKILLS	A specific example (or examples) where you have exercised this skill
Collecting numerical data: e.g., by measurement, observation and counting or from published data.	
Recording/understanding data in the form of tables or diagrams.	
Handling everyday numerical data, for example, fractions, decimals, mental arithmetic, multiplication tables and so on.	

Prompts: think about money as well as number – budgeting for yourself or others, working in a shop, restaurant or bar, running an ebay auction, working out commission and any aspect of your study that requires numerical work.

AWARENESS OF THE INDUSTRY	A specific example (or examples) where you have developed this awareness
Able to converse about current events relevant to film and media.	
Evidence of real and tangible interest in and commitment to the industry (or employer).	
Knowledge and opinion of some aspect of the industry.	
Real and relevant contact with one or more working environments.	

Prompts: actually creating or doing something will account for a lot in this section – from reading the media press to going to the cinema, logging reviews of concerts or getting involved in the student newspaper.

If, however, you couldn't find so many skills, do not despair. At least now you know what you have to work with. Treat the exercise as a checklist. Look at where the big gaps are and make sure you start to address them.

Some ideas to enhance employability

Do you want to, or think you may have to, work freelance or be self-employed? Lots of media people do know that this will be optional or inevitable. It is even more important for you to be aware of your employability because you will have to 'sell' your skills even more clearly to potential buyers. For example, an aspiring production researcher who makes sure she gains a good basis in administrative and office skills will be able to get temporary work fairly easily in between those plum research jobs. You must be flexible and prepared to work where and when you can. Employability really is about maximising your chances of getting where you want to be.

TIP

Other people who know you might have a clearer idea than you of what your skills, strengths and weaknesses are. Ask your family and friends for their honest opinions – you might be surprised.

So now we hope you have an understanding of the employability skills you already possess. What you can do with this information is build your employability still further in order to maximise your chances of success.

Building on your employability

The world of work has changed very rapidly in the last 50 years. Once, people could train for a job, leave school or college and be happily employed in the same work all their lives. In 1950 the vast majority of workers stayed in the first company or job they got. Nowadays, people are expected to change their career (not just their job) at least five times in their working lives. A job for life is almost completely unknown now. In the fields of media and film, it's probably never been like that except for a very few lucky ones. Because the working world is far less stable, it is really important to keep up-dated and to reconsider continually where you are in your life and career. You can't think of your employability skills as a set characteristics, like the colour of your eyes; you have to think of yourself as a product under continual renewal and improvement, reacting to what is happening around you.

Case study: Bill

An example of continued assessment is Bill, who left university with a joint degree in Film and English, having taken part enthusiastically in all the theatrical productions he could whilst studying. He applied to film companies all over the UK, hoping to get a break as a director, but without success. Eventually he took a part-time, temporary job in a museum, basically taking tickets, working in the gift shop and helping to organise events. After a few months a permanent job came up in the same museum and, somewhat reluctantly, he took it. It wasn't exactly his dream role but he worked well and enjoyed the ambiance of the museum and the teamwork involved. He got to know people in museums in the region through attending planning meetings. When a museum in a nearby town advertised on an internal bulletin for someone to take charge of an inner city heritage exhibition, which included directing short films to enhance historic displays, guess who got the job. Bill is now happily engaged as a heritage film manager and has become something of an expert in the field – and he even gets opportunities to direct.

Building your employability takes a bit of effort, but it is also something which is very likely to come fairly naturally to people wanting to work in the media. You are probably enthusiastic about your area of work. Maybe you love radio, film, history or books and will naturally read about the subject. You will probably want to know what's going on in your profession, even if it is gossip or articles about your favourite personalities. This all adds to your knowledge and makes you more employable.

You can also deliberately set out to make yourself more desirable both as a potential employee and as a freelance or self-employed professional. Here are some practical examples of how to bridge those skills gaps:

In film and the media it is especially important to be aware that learning is for life (sometimes referred to as 'Lifelong Learning'). Never be afraid to try something new, to learn something new. Even if you aren't great at something, employers will be impressed that you have tried.

Weak area	How to develop skills
IT	Build skills by taking ECDL (European Computer Driving Licence, often offered at local night schools and colleges) or CLAIT (a computer qualification, available at three levels, from beginners to advanced, and offered at colleges and by distance learning). Or do a skills swop – get a techie friend to tutor you in exchange for something you can do.
Business knowledge	If you already have a part-time job, explore what opportunities there are within your company to help you to understand business cultures. Could you shadow your supervisor for a day? Are there training courses you could attend, or could you interview a manager?

Case study: Kate

Kate is in her early fifties and has a passion for media. She worked in the Civil Service and had what most people would describe as a good job; she was well paid and had a good pension to look forward to. She was disabled and also caring for a husband with health problems, but despite these apparent handicaps Kate gave up her job and went to university to study film. She worked very hard and became something of a mother figure to many of the young people on the course. Kate got involved in everything she could at university. Her enthusiasm and dedication meant that she finished up with a good degree, albeit a little later than her co-students. Kate was pretty convinced that she would never get a job in the media – she felt she was unemployable. But she was wrong. Her commitment to lifelong self-improvement and learning impressed the BBC and she was offered a work placement in one of the regional studios.

TIP

Keep building on your employability skills. Be honest with yourself, work on your strengths to make them even better and look at your weak areas to see if there is anything you can do to improve.

So now you have an idea of how to build on your employability skills.

Notes for teachers

Individuals need to have a clear picture of their employability skills. They also need to record them. This will greatly help them to make more informed choices and better applications. It is worth spending time to help them to audit these skills in class or tutorials. Many students also welcome a 'reality check' to help them to identify how good they really are and how they can enhance their chances.

- Groups can collect and collate occupational information identifying examples of skills being required for work.
- Use the employability audit in whole or in parts for individuals to gather information about their skills.
- In pairs or triads, have students discuss each skill set to help them find new examples or enhance the examples they have identified.
- Individually or in groups, have them brainstorm imaginative ways they could enhance each of the skill sections.
- Role play interviewing each other with the skills as a checklist so students get accustomed to articulating and owning the skills.

FOUR Networking, promoting yourself and negotiation

By the end of this chapter you will know more about:

- How to establish a network
- How to promote yourself by 'looking the part'
- How to invest in yourself
- How to be assertive
- How to negotiate

This chapter looks at self-promotion, from presenting yourself outwardly as positively as possible to learning to become more assertive and negotiating effectively. It starts by introducing networking, that is, utilising others to promote yourself, how to establish a network and how to use your network effectively. You will find out some of the tactics used by our recent graduates and see why this aspect of career management is so crucial to your success.

Self-promotion is not only a really useful life skill; in terms of finding work in the media and culture industries, it is an absolutely fundamental tool to secure yourself an inroad. As you progress in your career you need to know how to promote yourself and maintain an advantage in the increasingly competitive workplace.

Establishing a network

One of the most important employability skills you can develop whilst still at university or college is *networking*. This is because networking allows you to present yourself in a much more personal way than a CV or standard job application form can ever do. Many of the jobs you will be hoping to find are not even likely to be advertised in the first place. This is because media jobs are frequently filled by 'word of mouth'. This doesn't mean that you don't need to take the trouble to write a good CV; what it does mean is that you need to make yourself visible and stand out in peoples' minds. If you make an impact, when a vacancy or other opportunity comes up, you will be remembered. Bearing this in mind, you need always to be very careful about how you present yourself to others. An informal remark made at a media event or in a casual encounter could easily be misinterpreted, so you need to exercise your judgement and aim to make a good impression.

Networking is also an absolutely fundamental activity for anyone who intends to work in a self-employed capacity. Freelance working or self-employment, combined with strong entrepreneurial skills, allow those who are passionate about the media to create their own films, videos or programmes with like-minded others. This way of working is becoming more and more common, and many production companies are run by small groups of individuals who have got together by networking. Whilst you may not currently believe you have got what it takes to work in a self-employed capacity, it is likely that you will consider this as an option in the future.

Now that you know that networking is important, let's look at how to go about constructing your own personal network.

1. Who do you know NOW? Who do the people you know KNOW? You can begin your network by deciding which companies or organisations you would like to work for and which individuals you would like to meet. Draw up a list and then carry out some research.
2. Find out as much as you can about the overall aims of the organisation and what they are currently doing. Try to identify key individuals and write down a mini-biography which you may need to use at a later date to jog your memory.
3. Have a set of cards made with your name, address and contact details plus a line or two about yourself and what you have to offer. Practice saying it as a one minute 'pitch'.
4. Attend any events which are related to your chosen area of work/interest. These might include media career fairs and recruitment drives, sector skills events and industry open days. Look out, too, for casual opportunities at parties, clubs, bars and network with friends and family who may also know people who are working in your chosen career.
5. Take advantage of any work placements or work experience opportunities which present you with people to add to your network.
6. Take the names and contact details of any guest speakers who give a presentation at university or college.

If you follow these steps you should have a good set of contacts within your network.

Next you need to take things a step further by bringing your network to life – a long list of names in a diary will not help you to find your dream job. Develop the habit of self-promotion by offering your card to people within your network. You could also create your own web page and add to it any of your achievements and some details about your ambitions. Make use of existing web networking resources such as myspace. Email or telephone anyone interesting who took the trouble to speak to you and thank them for their time. It is also a good idea to remind them of your interests and ask them to keep you in mind should they need support in the future. You can repeat this exercise again 6–12 months later, but try to use judgement. Forcing people to take notice of you will only create an impression of desperation. If your efforts are not welcomed, then you need to show sensitivity and respect and keep your distance.

Keep track of your network and make sure you update it regularly. It is also a good idea to continually update your research about those within your network to avoid potential embarrassment and to increase your confidence in communicating effectively.

Some examples of effective networking

1. A guest speaker comes to your university to talk about careers in radio. Make sure that you try to speak to them at the end of the session. Introduce yourself clearly and confidently. Follow this by saying how much you enjoyed the talk. Tell them what you would like to do and ask if they can give you any suggestions as to how to further your career. Offer thanks for any advice, give them your card and ask if it would be alright to call them in the future. Don't forget to make that phone call.
2. You are offered two weeks' work experience as a runner on a television production. Ensure that you make a positive impression on people who you meet by carrying out your duties efficiently and politely and offering to help out over and above the call of duty. When opportunities arise, ask for email addresses and phone numbers and remember to offer your contact details too. Make sure that you thank your employer and colleagues for the experience. Finally, let it be known that you are keen to secure a permanent job when you graduate and that you would also be keen to obtain further work experience if any becomes available. Follow this up with a letter of thanks and a further reminder, asking for your details to be kept on file.
3. You identify some interesting jobs for picture researchers, all of which appeal to you but all of which state that they wish to recruit someone with work experience. Write letter of introduction

to these companies and ask if they would be able to help you to break into this field of employment by giving you some work experience (paid or unpaid). Follow up your letter with a polite phone call, and don't be deterred if your efforts fail on this occasion.

Self-promotion – looking the part

If you want to maximise your impact on others, you need to give consideration to making the most of your appearance. Whilst some will always argue that valuing others by their looks and clothing is essentially shallow, we live in a society which places considerable emphasis on the importance of appearances. As the sociologist of human interaction (Goffman 1956: 28) argued in his seminal work *The Presentation of Self in Everyday Life:* 'When an individual plays a part he implicitly requests his observers to take seriously the impression that is fostered before them.'

This is because the image which we promote to others becomes synonymous with ourselves and thus great care must be taken to create a favourable impression. This does not mean that only the best looking and expensively dressed can find employment. It doesn't even mean that you have to change yourself radically. What it means is that you have to make the most of yourself in the all important situations where you interact face-to-face with others or in any photographs you may include in letters of introduction or CVs. Evidence indicates that employers make up their mind about individual candidates for a job within the first *minute* of a personal encounter.

What follows reinforces this viewpoint. This is sometimes called the 'halo effect'. So how do we make sure we 'look the part'?

Investing in yourself

Many of us find it difficult to even think about investing time and money in ourselves. This can be simply due to lack of finances, but it can also be due to low self-esteem. If you don't believe you are worthy, then you need to question some of the assumptions you are making about yourself. There are very good reasons why you should invest time and money in yourself. First, if you invest in improving your appearance, you could get a better-paid job, and secondly, by doing so you can raise your self-esteem, giving you more confidence at interview.

Even if you are working with a low budget you can find ways to invest in yourself. In order to make the most of yourself you need to take a serious inventory of your best and worst qualities. Ask friends and family to help you to compile a list of your strongest points; for example, hair, eyes, smile, sense of humour, warmth. Then look at what you consider to be your weakest points. Finally, try to establish which aspects of yourself you can change in order to give a strong and positive impression.

Examples from our work with students include:

1. Changing the tone and character of the voice. Some of our students have found that they can turn a flat, excessively quiet and hesitant tone of voice into a much stronger and positive tool for communication. This can be achieved in just two sessions with an experienced vocal coach. Good books are:

    > Denny, R. (2006) *Communicate to Win*. London: Kogan Page.
    > Hughes, D. (2000) *The Oxford Union Guide to Successful Public Speaking*. London: Virgin Books.
    > Maggion, R. (2005) *The Art of Talking to Anyone: Essential People Skills for Success in Any Situation*. London: McGraw-Hill.

2. Updating an old-fashioned and unattractive dress sense into a much more funky, up-to-date style. You can study fashion magazines, ask friends or, if finances allow, invest in a session with a professional stylist. There are also some useful books on the subject of dress code and the impact you make by wearing certain colours and styles. Try:

    > Molloy, J. (1996) *New Women's Dress for Success*. New York: Warner.
    > Sampson, E. (1996) *The Image Factor – A Guide to Self-presentation for Career Enhancement*. London: Kogan Page.
    > Taylor, R. (2000) *Transform Yourself*. London: Kogan Page.

3. Work on improving the message that your body language is giving. If you come across as unassertive and lacking in confidence, your body language is usually one of the main cues. This is a behaviour which you can change. There are a number of helpful books around which could help you to create a more confident image:

    > Goldman, E. (2004) *As Others See Us: Body Movement and the Art of Successful Communication*: New York: Routledge.
    > James, J. (2001) *Bodytalk at Work: How to Use Effective Body Language to Boost Your Career*. London: Piatkus.
    > Pease, A. and Pease, B. (2004) *The Definitive Book of Body Language*. London: Orion.

If you feel and look the part you want to play, you have much more chance of actually achieving it by sending out the right, positive signals to employers, clients and colleagues.

Self-promotion – assertiveness

Many students in our careers management workshops make the mistake of confusing aggressiveness with assertiveness. Being assertive doesn't have to mean dominating in a group, it doesn't mean being the loudest or pushiest, and it certainly doesn't mean bullying others and coercing them into following your wishes. Assertiveness can help you to achieve goals such as:

- Standing up for your rights when you believe you are being bullied.
- Enabling you to resist being pressured to conform to wishes of other, more dominant people.
- Maintaining your right to express beliefs and opinions while respecting the beliefs and opinions of others.

If you are not sure whether or not you need to be more assertive, ask yourself if any of the following apply to you:

- You find it difficult to say no and if you do say it, you doubt that you have a right to say it.
- You avoid saying what you really feel and bottle up your feelings until they explode later on.
- You worry about failure to the point that you won't even try to do something new or challenging.
- You think that nobody listens to you when you are trying to put forward your ideas and thoughts.
- You often give in to other, more dominant people.

If you feel that you identify strongly with these statements, you will certainly benefit from becoming more assertive. This is not going to mean that you must automatically shout in a group situation or erupt with fury when someone upsets you rather than bottle-up your feelings. It means that you are going to learn how to make yourself clear and avoid being pushed into doing things you do not wish to do if you believe that the demands are unreasonable.

Here are a few brief tips on how to assert yourself. If you wish to find out more, there are some good self-help books on the subject, and you could attend an assertiveness training workshop.

Some techniques to increase assertiveness

1. **Establish what it is that you want to achieve.**
   Unless you do this, you will not be able even to begin to assert yourself. If you have no clear idea of an ideal outcome, your

uncertainty will be picked up by others and this will undermine your efforts. Think carefully about what you would like to happen. Examples might include: stopping a friend from putting you down; making sure that people listen to you when you speak in a group setting; and saying no to someone who keeps asking you to do things you don't want to do.

2. **Get your facts right.**
   Find out all that you can regarding the facts of the situation so that you are thoroughly prepared. This means that if you are unhappy that your friend makes disparaging comments about you, you must record the details of when and where these things were said and in what context. You should also write down how these comments are affecting you, using clear and non-judgemental language.

Example

A fellow student (Louise) doesn't make any effort to contribute to a forthcoming group seminar presentation, the deadline is looming and her failure to contribute is going to put pressure on the rest of the group and may lead to you losing marks. Sarah is feeling angry and frustrated about it. She could begin by approaching Louise like this:

> 'We have a presentation in two weeks' time. We agreed at the beginning of term that we would all contribute and you said that you would do the section on audience statistics. We need this input now if we are to achieve the deadline without losing marks.'
>
> 'If we lose marks this will affect our results in the second year. I don't know how you feel about this, but I am worried because I want to get a good mark for this part of the course. I am unhappy that we can't complete the presentation without your work.'

Then establish what you would like to happen in future, again using plain, simple and non-judgemental words:

> 'Please tell me if you have done the work and when it will be ready.'

Be prepared for a reaction

By establishing what you are unhappy about and saying what you want to happen, you have already started to assert your needs. However, you don't have any control over the response you will get, so you should prepare yourself in advance by using your imagination and thinking about what will be said in reply.

Here are some possible responses from Louise:

'I've been trying to get the work done. I'm doing my best, stop going on about it.'

'Nick hasn't finished his contribution either but you aren't nagging him, are you?'

'Nobody will tell me where to start. I'm sick of this. If you're so bothered, why don't you do it?'

'Don't worry, I have done it. I just need to email it to everyone.'

If you have an idea of some of the less helpful responses you might anticipate, you can work on trying out a few assertive replies. Again, choose your words carefully, stick to the point and don't allow yourself to be pushed into backing down. This may include asking for further clarification, restating the question or making a challenge. Avoid using emotive language and don't respond to rude comments with further abuse. You may feel afraid or lack faith in your rights when a more dominant individual continues to try to assert their needs over yours. The main thing to remember is that if you maintain your standpoint and continue to be firm, the bullying will not work.

'I appreciate that you are trying to get the work done. When will it be ready? Can you be more precise?'

'I am concerned to find out where *you* are up to with the work. I will speak to Nick next.'

'We agreed that we would each take on the work which was allocated. I am not prepared to do this as well as my own contribution. If you need help, the tutor is the best person to ask.'

'Brilliant! Can you email it to me tonight and we can all meet to finish the presentation tomorrow?'

Stand firm

Hopefully this will do the trick, but you may find that your attempts to assert yourself are met with downright abuse or a refusal to cooperate or some other negative response. Try not to be disheartened. Stick by your principles. If you tend to be submissive, this will be difficult initially, but with practice you will find it easier to maintain your position. If you find that your request is dismissed, ignored or you receive abuse, then you can simply restate it or indicate that you are not prepared to accept such treatment. Avoid shouting or losing your cool and, if necessary, walk away.

At least if you make your point, this in itself often helps to make others respect you more in the long run. You may find that you have to walk away from some situations but you may not be seen as such a pushover in future now that you have shown you are prepared to speak up for yourself. Try to learn from each situation and use strategies which will lead to a more positive outcome in future. This could mean spelling things out more clearly to friends, colleagues or family and making your boundaries clearer from the outset.

Watch your body language

If you intend to assert yourself, you must also pay attention to your body language. How you say things and how you look are often more important to others than what you say. The message will be much more effective if you use an open, upright posture and steady eye contact. Make sure that you sound as though you mean business by speaking clearly and forcefully. People tend to take others less seriously if they whisper, mumble and stand in a submissive position. You have to start believing in yourself and your rights otherwise nobody else will. A good technique is to rehearse your requests out loud in front of the mirror or before an understanding friend who will give you honest feedback on the credibility of your voice and body language.

Assertiveness will be a very useful tool in your future career and life itself, so get used to practising and improving the skills as soon as you can. Start today.

Negotiating

This is where your assertiveness skills need to be used to the most advantage. You will need to start learning to negotiate if you are going to take charge of your career. When opportunities come your way you should try to make the most of them by asking for what you want. Negotiating skills can be used in all of the following situations:

- when trying to establish what you would like to achieve from work experience;
- when asking if you can modify or change the conditions of a work placement;
- when you would like a pay rise; and
- when you believe you are being asked to do too much or too little or if you think you are being asked to do something dangerous or unhealthy.

Where to start

Begin by thinking carefully about what it is you wish to achieve and write down or mentally rehearse saying this as clearly as possible to the person or people you wish to negotiate with.

Examples

You are offered some work experience with a local employer who has indicated that this will be unpaid. You are going to have to take time off from your paid part-time job in order to do the work experience and will be seriously out of pocket. This work experience is very important to you and you know that it is going to seriously improve your chances of finding a job later on.

Now look at all the outcome you would like from your negotiation and order them in terms of priority:

- You would like to be paid a wage.
- You would like some other financial support, for example, help with bus or rail fares and lunches.
- You would like them to consider allowing you to look at ways you could combine the placement with your part time job.

Make sure that you set up a sensible time to discuss the request with the appropriate member of staff. It is pointless trying to negotiate when someone is hell bent on leaving work to go on a prearranged evening out. Show respect and consideration for others if you wish the same for yourself. Don't waste time building up to saying what is on your mind, particularly if this is going to be difficult. State your request politely and positively. Explain your position and indicate what it is that you would like them to consider. Ask the person if they need time to think and if so, set up a further meeting.

> 'I would really like to do this placement and I know you said at the interview that it would be unpaid. Would you be prepared to reconsider this at all? I am really keen to do the work, but now that I have had a chance to look at the finances, I know it would be difficult to give up the income from my part-time job.'

You may meet with a negative response and if so, you can continue to try to negotiate:

> 'If you can't pay me a wage, then would you consider paying my expenses? It would cost around £55 a week for bus fares and lunches.'
>   or

'Alternatively, would it be possible for me to work the hours around my part-time paid job? This placement is so important to me and I really do want it.'

Self-promotion, assertiveness and skills of negotiation may not come easily to us, but with practice you can learn how to make the most of yourself and stand up for yourself. Take advantage of any opportunities for self-development: courses and workshops at university, training sessions at work or on placement, evening classes, books and DVDs. Keep a record of your progress, such as a daily diary or relevant events, so that you can see how well you are doing and be determined to continue to develop. Being assertive and aware are skills that will help you not only in work, but also in life generally.

Notes for teachers

Learning to build a network, be assertive and to negotiate are vital skills that will help anybody develop their career and be more successful in life generally. Introducing these concepts to students will help them to develop understanding of how their behaviour can impact upon their success in study, work and life in general.

- Students create a 'personal network map' in the form of a mind map with self at the centre. Branching out from the centre are different aspects of their life. They identify people they know (or are aware of) in each of these aspects. They can discuss and share their networks with each other.
- Students may work in pairs to explore assertiveness. One student takes on the role of a potential employee, the other to be the employer. The potential employee has to negotiate the timing of a work placement so that it will fit in with their university timetable, whilst the employer negotiates the maximum hours he can from the employee.
- Role play a scenario at university where two students are regularly leaving a third to carry out the lion's share of the workload for a joint presentation.
- Put students in groups and let them take it in turns to deliver a pre-written request in an assertive or submissive manner. Ask them to reflect on the process.

FIVE   Work experience – the key to success

By the end of this chapter you will know more about:

- What is relevant work experience and how to get it
- How to make the most of your work experience

We cannot emphasise too much how important it is for you to get relevant and meaningful experience to add to your academic study. Even if you don't apply any of the other advice offered in this book, you will hugely improve your career chances just by doing this one thing. This chapter links to the last one regarding building your network because one of the key ways you can build your network is by putting yourself forward for experiences that give you an extra lift into the competitive job market. It links to the next chapter on applying for work, because without relevant work experience you will struggle to produce a decent winning application.

What is work experience?

This may seem an obvious question, but students and graduates can sometimes have a limited view of what work experience really is. It can be interpreted in many different ways and there are many hidden opportunities to gain experience that may not be apparent at first glance. In fact, some assumptions about what work experience is can actually put people off getting it.

- **Assumption 1: it takes up too much time**
  Work experience does not have to take a long time. It does not have to last for a year, a month, two weeks, one week or even a full day. Half a day or a few hours in the right environment can

be a highly useful and focussed experience that will help you to see whether a job is right for you and whether you are right for it. It can also be impressive on an application form to show you have done lots of mini-experiences.

- **Assumption 2: it has to be with a big, well-known employer**
  Of course it would be great if we could all get work experience with Channel 4 or the *Sunday Times* – and some of us may do just that – but realistically this isn't available to most of us. You are already aware from Chapter 2 that there are a lot more small- and medium-sized employers, freelancers and self-employed people in the media related industries, and they will offer different, and equally valid, work experiences.
- **Assumption 3: it is really difficult to arrange**
  Yes, it requires some confidence, some energy and some commitment to arrange work experience, but if you don't have these qualities you are going to find it very difficult to get into a competitive career anyway. You should treat obtaining work experience as a dry run for getting a real job and put in the time and effort – it will pay off. Many people get real jobs directly through work experience, so it is well worth the effort. Check the assertiveness section of Chapter 4 for tips on how to approach work experience providers.
- **Assumption 4: you have to be able to do the job already**
  For work experience to be valuable, you don't necessarily have to be actually doing the job. Consider 'work shadowing' for high-skill, high-profile careers. Work shadowing simply means organising an opportunity to observe closely or interview a professional. This will be impressive to a potential employer who knows full well that you haven't had the chance to direct a television programme or write a novel. It can also give you a fantastic insight into the realities of your fantasy role.

So work experience can be for a short space of time, it can be with any size and status of employer or freelancer, and it can be arranged with a well-planned telephone call, email or letter. Work shadowing and other exposures to working life can be just as valuable.

But what about relevance – what exactly is *relevant* work experience?

There is no point in spending a lot of time and energy on getting yourself work experience in something that isn't going to really give you added value. This means that you must go for something meaningful *for you*. Remember everything we said in Chapter 1 about employability? Your skills audit will have indicated some areas that you could work on to enhance your overall employability. This should be your first priority in terms of work experience.

Let's look at an example

Salma is a final year media student who would love to work in magazines but has no relevant experience. Her employability audit revealed that she lacks awareness of the industry and is weak in creativity and problem solving – also it is a long time since she dealt with numbers, so her numeracy isn't up to much.

How can work experience help Salma?

Her first thought was how great it would be to get a two-week placement in *Hello* magazine, but that seemed a bit daunting to arrange. So she looked through the local *Yellow Pages* and asked her tutors if any of them could suggest a magazine where she could work. The husband of one of her tutors worked in a large company that had its own in-house magazine for employees. He was happy to ask a favour of a colleague who arranged for Salma to spend a Wednesday afternoon in the tiny office watching how it was put together. She was even invited to write a short article about being a student on placement in the company.

Then Salma thought about the creativity and problem-solving aspect of her employability. Where could she get some experience of that? Her sister worked part-time in an old people's home and suggested that Salma could do an activity with some of the old ladies – the staff were always looking for things to do to entertain them. Salma organised a fun pamper afternoon for the elderly female residents by approaching a local hairdresser and beauty therapist and begging some free products from a department store. She took photos and made an album for the staff, the residents of the home and their relatives. It didn't take too long and was fun to organise.

Salma thought about her weak numeracy but really couldn't be bothered looking for relevant work experience for that. Instead she decided to make a proper budget for her own spending. She found a simple computer program to do this and tried it over a month. It helped her to revise some number skills and she also managed to save a bit of money for a spree at the end of the month.

All this experience helped Salma to make a much stronger case for her own employability, gave her interesting things to write about on applications and talk about at interview, and did not cost her a great deal in terms of time and effort. She managed to integrate it all into her normal life of study and work – and had fun at the same time.

TIP

Why not get together with a friend or two and brainstorm some of the mad, wild or creative ways you could get relevant experience?

Voluntary work

There are many opportunities available for students and graduates to get direct access to volunteer work, much of which is extremely valuable. Many universities have their own volunteer organisations, for example community action groups, Millennium Volunteers, sports volunteering, mentoring (of pupils, students or people outside the institution), even opportunities to volunteer for experimental work in academic departments such as Psychology. Check with the students union if you are not sure what is available.

When you begin to explore the wider community, outside education, the potential is enormous. For example, many cities, towns and regions have interesting volunteer groups, some of which relate to their historic or natural environment. Details will be held by public libraries and are often available online. A national website offers a range of volunteer links (including media related, for instance volunteering at a radio station).

There would not be sufficient space in this entire book to describe all the excellent volunteer schemes there are throughout the UK, Europe and beyond. A good place to start looking is the volunteer section of your university careers library (or electronic library) which will hold details of hundreds of volunteer projects and organisations (see, for example, www.do-it.org.uk). And don't think you have to sign your life away for years at a time; there are one-off projects, short-term and long-term volunteering options, as well as things that you can do on a weekly or ad-hoc basis.

Don't worry if the opportunity is not in a career area of interest to you – think about the transferable, employability skills you can develop when you choose your volunteer work. That is much more important than the detail of the tasks you undertake.

Some of the benefits of undertaking voluntary work are:

- You will almost certainly learn new things outside the comfort zone of academic study or part-time jobs
- You will meet a whole new set of people, either as co-volunteers or clients, or both.
- You will almost certainly grow in confidence and maturity.

- You will probably have a lot of fun – and if it isn't fun, at least you can prove your resilience and perseverance – very useful for media careers.
- You will impress employers by showing initiative and interest in others, signified through volunteering.

Why work experience is so important

Work experience is important because it will often lead to real, paid, satisfying jobs and careers. There is nothing more convincing, at interview or application stage or when pitching for work, to have positive proof that you can do the job – and great work experience can give you this proof. Employers value work experience. Read what Ian Pearman, who recruits for one of the world's largest advertising agencies, says:

> Many graduates lack even the most basic of interpersonal skills … the breadth of knowledge required of our graduates is so much wider than ever before. They need to understand that we are a business. It's not just about producing award-winning commercials, it's also about revenue and profits. That's why between 30–50 per cent of our new hirings [employees] are people who had the motivation to participate in some work experience. (Pearman, 2005: 15)

Work experience can give you an abundance of skills, aptitudes, contacts and confidence *if* you manage it effectively. You are probably one of the vast majority of students who hold down part-time jobs already. Do not feel you have to stick in one job too long; once you have learnt what you can from it, move on. Don't allow yourself to become too comfortable or be too loyal to change your job. Look for an opportunity to do something different and so enhance your skills, even if it's something that you wouldn't naturally be drawn to. It is all about pushing your comfort zone and trying new things.

So any work experience, work shadowing, observation, short courses, conference attendance and voluntary activities can be included in your work experience portfolio, and this will give you an enormous advantage in the market place.

How to find work experience

There are many ways of finding work experience, depending on what you have decided to go for. The first principle is to be clear and structured about what you want. The clearer you are, the easier it will be for others to understand and help you. Planning is important in all aspects of career decision making and it is absolutely vital to enable you to find appropriate, useful and interesting experience.

An obvious place to start from is something in your immediate environment. There are usually quite a few temporary or part-time jobs around for students (and recent graduates). Your university may have one of the increasing number of 'job shops' which frequently carry unusual and off-beat vacancies from organisations that specifically target students. Taking up an opportunity like this can give you a skill set that you would not otherwise gain and which other people might find it hard to offer, which in turn can enhance your job potential to employers.

Think about what exactly you want before you approach anyone – although of course, you need to be a bit flexible too.

Julien's search for work experience

Julien isn't sure about exactly what he wants to do, but he knows he 'would like to work with others in something creative, maybe publishing'. He decided to make a plan to help him think about what he needed from work experience and how to get it. First he looked at his work experience needs based on his employability audit:

1. IT – my skills are pretty weak except in word processing and Internet search.
2. I have had no experience of getting anything published.
3. I get nervous and stutter when giving presentations.

Julien already had a part-time job stacking shelves at night in a supermarket. Before that he had a paper round and helped in a dairy. He thought about *networking* with contacts who could help him:

'Lots of staff in the University department have published books. My colleagues at work, Mum's contacts at work in the HR office where she is based.'

He then made a work experience plan:

1. To improve my IT skills by learning at least three Microsoft programs by the end of summer.
2. To get something that I have written published somewhere before I leave uni.
3. To improve my oral communication skills and be more confident in front of groups within a year.
4. To do some project work with at least three other people that is creative or related.

(Continued)

(Continued)

You can see that already Julien has become much clearer about what he really needs and wants from work experience to help him to improve his employability skills. This planning almost immediately suggested some possible options for getting the skills and experience he needed:

'Marc at work is an absolute computer wiz and I am sure would help me work through examples and improve my IT skills. In exchange I can help him with written English if he wants to apply for jobs.'

'I am going to ask my lecturers for suggestions for the kinds of articles that I could get published – I know that some final years and postgraduates in the department have done this, so it can't be impossible.'

'Stacking shelves is not improving my confidence or spoken skills – I am going to ask my manager for till training or look for another job dealing with the public.'

This is all targeted, bona fide and relevant work experience. Just having the new skills Julien develops will be useful to him in employment search, but perhaps more than this, the fact that he has taken such a proactive, organised approach to his own development will give him a massive advantage over those who drift aimlessly. It will be a great help when he comes to write applications.

TIP

Create your own plan to see what opportunities you might have to develop interesting and relevant work experiences.

In the previous chapter, we suggested creating a list or plan of your network which should have expanded your potential range of relations and contacts. This is a good place to start. If you haven't made a list of contacts this yet, do so before you move on.

There are standard ways of looking for work experience – check this list to make sure you have considered them all:

Resource

☑ University job shop
☑ University Careers Service
☑ Jobcentre Plus (online)
☑ Local Jobcentre (part of Dept for Work and Pensions)
☑ Local recruitment agencies (check *Yellow Pages*)
☑ National recruitment agencies
☑ Local newspapers
☑ National newspapers
☑ Specialist journals/press
☑ Magazines
☑ Lecturers in your department
☑ Placement offices in colleges and universities
☑ Noticeboards and department offices
☑ Vacancy newspapers
☑ Graduate sections in newspapers
☑ Graduate directories (often available from careers offices)
☑ Business directories (reference libraries have these)
☑ Graduate vacancy and placement websites

There may be other less conventional approaches too:

Method

☑ Write directly to a famous person or top name in the field
☑ Contact through an electronic group – check Google groups to start
☑ Respond to an article or editorial in a newspaper or journal
☑ Ask your careers adviser to suggest or source a contact
☑ Contact lecturers outside your department or university
☑ Go abroad – contact international agencies for opportunities
☑ Write an open letter to a national magazine or newspaper asking for help
☑ Community groups – libraries have lists of these
☑ Approach the Chamber of Trade or employer representative organisations
☑ Write to unions and trade groups
☑ Telephone companies direct, using *Yellow Pages* for the nearest big town or business centre

☑ Make a leaflet and take it or post it to companies
☑ Make a business card or flyer about what you want and hand it to delegates at conferences, festivals or events

Making the most of your work experience

There are two main ways to make the most of any work experience you can get. The first and primary aim is to ensure that you learn as much as you can, as quickly as you can. The second is to ensure that you meet as many people as possible and make a good impression upon them. Again, as you might expect, planning is the key to success.

Before going on work experience

Think about what you want to gain from the work experience, make a few notes and discuss this with your provider. If this is not feasible, at least make your own list of what you want to get out of it. For example, you might want to learn about how an office works, observe a team meeting, visit a certain department, talk to a specific type of professional or do a particular task. Be clear, polite and flexible. Negotiate rather than demand, and be ready to adapt to what your provider can give.

Whilst you are on work experience

No matter what length of time you have in any work experience, keep a record of what you learn and the people you meet. Take a notebook and make sure you jot down all useful information, names, telephone numbers, email addresses, resources, company names and anything else that might be helpful. Ask everyone you meet whether it's OK to take their details, and be sure to thank them. It can be useful to ask people you meet for advice related to your own plans. For instance, you could ask how they got their role, what they think are the best and worst aspects of their job, what advice they had before they entered their career, and what they hope to go on to in the future. Be friendly and make conversation rather than treating it like an interview. Most people are genuinely happy to talk about themselves and their work and are generally willing to talk to newbies. But do also be aware that people are, in the main, extremely busy and often harassed at work. Ask if it is a convenient time and be prepared to make appointments later if they are pressed. Always be prepared to offer to buy a coffee.

After work experience

It is a old-fashioned courtesy to thank people after a visit of whatever length by a small gesture such as a telephone call or a little card, even an email if that's all you can manage. In any case do thank your provider (and any other people who have been particularly helpful) one way or another. A card and/or a gift for the office, such as a plant or box of biscuits, will help people remember you. For yourself you should read over your notes, reflect on what you have learnt, follow up any contacts and file your information so you can access it rapidly. If you are hoping to use the experience to get you into a job, it is really important to ask someone with authority whether they might be prepared to write a reference for you in the future. Make sure you have the details you will need to provide if they agree. If they do not want to act as a referee, they may be willing to write a brief testimonial for you.

TIP

Create a data base of contacts which you can update regularly. It could be a little black book, a pretty notepad or an Excel workbook – whatever you like.

Rights, responsibilities, safety and health

Many of you will already be working and be well aware of health and safety issues and how important these are. For work experience, you may be going into environments that are inherently unsafe. This may be anywhere from a police station to a film set, a hospital to a newspaper office. Wherever you are, and especially when you are on work experience, be extra careful about your own health and safety.

The vast majority of organisations will have employers' liability insurance and/or public liability insurance, but it would be perfectly acceptable to check this with them. If it is not mentioned by the provider you can enquire, 'Is there anything I need to do to cover health and safety?' When you are on work experience, you should be treated exactly as if you were an employee as regards safety, and you also have the same responsibilities to ensure your own safety and that of colleagues and the public. The Health and Safety Executive has useful information on its website (www.hse.gov.uk/) and you should consult this if you have any worries at all in this regard.

Working behind the scenes can be exciting

Never tackle any task or do anything that you believe could be dangerous or risky to yourself or others whilst on work experience. Go by your instinct.

Another consideration is the importance of confidentiality. This doesn't just include avoiding gossiping about colleagues or bosses, it also means being aware that professionals and companies want to hold onto their intellectual copyright and not give away useful information to competitors. This is particularly true in fields such as media, film, journalism and similar, where ideas equate with income. So be discreet and careful about this aspect. You could even mention it when negotiating work experience: 'Of course, I will respect confidentiality whilst I am with you and afterwards.'

Unpaid working and pricing yourself

Some people feel very uncomfortable about the idea of working for free. You must think this through yourself and if you feel exploited or uncomfortable about anything you are expected or asked to do, you should say so. If the worst comes to the worst you can politely withdraw, but these scenarios are very unlikely. The main principle to keep in mind is that you are really in a position of learning, which is equivalent to the company offering you training – and training costs a lot of money. It could be argued that you should be paying them.

You or an employer may also be concerned about the implications of taking jobs from other people whilst you are undertaking work experience. You certainly will not want to feel that professionals are losing out on proper work just because you need the experience. Be reassured that in the vast number of cases you will not be competing in any way with real professionals. It is most unlikely that you could replicate their skills and experience. Remember, too, that they all started at the bottom, and someone probably helped them to get a foot on the first rung of the ladder.

Work experience in your career portfolio

There is absolutely no point in undertaking any kind of work experience at all unless you know how to use it to get into the career of your choice. No matter how much you enjoy it, or how hard you work, the real test of relevant work experience is how far it pushes you in the direction you want to go.

You must include work experience in your written and verbal applications, and there are a number of ways of approaching this:

- **On your Curriculum Vitae**: We will talk about CVs in the next chapter, but make sure that you put the most relevant work you have done on the first page of your two-page document. You can describe the tasks that you did, or the skills that you gained, or both.
- **In application forms**: Questions on application forms can be answered by drawing on incidents, tasks, activities or roles that you have had through your work experience. Very often applications ask for examples of challenges you have overcome and experiences of 'leadership' or 'teamwork'. Finding examples of this from work experience will liven up your form and enhance your application greatly in the eyes of the recruiter.
- **At interview**: Make sure you include your work experience at interview – the interviewer may not prompt you but you should make sure that at some point you mention your experiences. If they are skilful, the interviewer will go on to probe you about this.
- **Speculative applications**: When approaching other employers or individuals, tell them about your experience and link it to why

you want to work for them. Evidence that you have done work previously helps people feel confident about employing you or offering further experiences.

Next steps – applications

The next chapters take you through the process of transforming your employability skills, career plans and work experience into that all-important first job.

Notes for teachers

You can support students in their search for meaningful work experiences that will enable them to develop career-related and transferable skills.

- Building from their individual network, create a group network in which students map their contacts and employer experience in small teams and then as a group to create a 'class network' diagram, folder or electronic resource.
- Ask work experience providers and/or placement staff to visit the group to offer advice and guidance specifically in work experience.
- Individually or in groups, have them brainstorm imaginative ways they could approach potential work providers.
- Practice cold-calling potential contacts using a tape recorder, dictaphone or verbal role plays.

SIX   Applications – first steps

By the end of this chapter you will know more about:

- How to make career decisions
- How to sell yourself to employers
- How to research jobs
- How to make speculative applications
- How to prepare application forms
- Making a career action plan

The next two chapters are all about getting a real job. Much of the guidance in previous chapters is really a preparation for this, so make sure you have understood it before you attempt to implement the advice that follows. The work experience chapter links particularly closely to these chapters because the process of finding and obtaining work experience is almost the same as that for real paid work. Although we cite examples primarily from film and media, the information applies equally to other employment fields.

This chapter informs you about conventional applications which are usually made in response to a posted vacancy, including application forms, online applications, curriculum vitae, letters, selection procedures and formal interviews. The next chapter uncovers the so-called 'hidden' opportunities using more creative and unconventional approaches: speculative applications, email, pitching, presentations, telephone interviews and portfolios. Both may be valuable at different times during your career and life.

Career decisions

Have you already made your career decision? Or are you considering more than one option? Perhaps you are completely undecided? Or maybe you don't even want to think about making a decision? All these positions are perfectly normal for someone in a stage of 'transition'.

There are a few tips that might help you with your career decisions and which might also help you with future important life decisions. One of the best places to start is from your own understanding of yourself. Consider the following three decision-making types and see which one feels most like you.

Type 1:

- Are you able to make decisions easily and confidently?
- Have you always been encouraged to make your own decisions and been supported when these went wrong?
- Have you experience of successful decision making or of coping well with the process of making important decisions? For example, you made your own choices about what and where to study, where to live or what to do in your free time.

If this seems like you, then you are probably a *decisive person* and should be able to manage effective decision making in the future.

Type 2:

- Are you often torn between options?
- Do you tend to see one side, then another, then yet another in any options?
- Do you tend to put off decision making and prefer to let decisions 'make themselves'? For example, did you find it difficult to choose subjects to study, university courses or locations, do you find it tricky to choose what to do on days off?

If this seems like you, then you may be an *indecisive person*, one who needs to think things through and practice decision making using various techniques.

Type 3:

- Do you get anxious and upset when forced to make a decision?
- Will you do anything to avoid making decisions and panic when you have made them?
- Do you look to others to make decisions for you? For example, do you lie awake and worry about decisions, even fairly minor ones, have you very few or no examples of making successful decisions in the past?

If this seems like you, you may be one of the small minority of people for whom *decision making itself is a problem*. You might want to consider getting support and guidance from a career practitioner, professional careers adviser, counsellor or coach. Your university will be able to refer you to a suitable person. If you are outside an institution you may need to approach advice centres or similar provision to get access to guidance.

Whatever 'type' you feel you may be, or even if you don't fit into any of these categories, there are simple techniques to help you to make decisions.

Information

Often, it is difficult to make decisions because we do not have enough data to base a decision on. Sometimes this will be insurmountable, but in careers this is very rare. Most of the decisions you need to make in careers will benefit from knowing more about you (self-awareness) and more about what's on offer in the world (sometimes called 'opportunity awareness'). Learn all you can about yourself: your strengths, interests, motivation, what you love and what makes you excited, what you dislike and what you are capable of. Learn also all you can about what might be out there for you by researching, reading, talking to others, taking work experience and job opportunities. This process can be a life-long adventure.

Head and heart

We tend to make decisions in two ways: using our rational, analytical brain and our more intuitive, gut instinct, what 'feels right'. People often have a preference for one or the other, but many find it useful to be aware of both. You could make a long list of 'pros' and 'cons' and still dismiss your analysis at the end of the day because your heart is pulling you in another direction. Or you might have been drawn to something and then when you rationally explore it, find it wouldn't suit you at all. Be aware of both your head and heart in decision making, utilising both aspects to make your conclusion.

Telling your story

Quite often the process of explaining or expounding your dilemma leads you to a decision which eluded you whilst you were alone. Being listened to in itself can help you make decisions, even if there is no guidance or advice available. Find suitable people to talk over decisions, whether these be family, friends or others.

Take a calculated risk

One of the major worries about career decisions is that somehow they will be irreversible and that you will set out on a totally inappropriate plan. In fact this is rarely the case. Most people at some time in their career make a 'wrong' move. Nearly always this provides a new perspective and an unexpected bonus – even if it is the realisation that pig farming definitely isn't for you or that you hate working shifts. Be aware that there is no set 'script' to work to; your career is a work in progress, a novel you are forever writing, a creative process that may take you anywhere. Learn to accept that risk is part of life and that sometimes there is no right answer; you have to trust the process. At the beginning of your career it will seem very daunting, but career decision making, like most decisions in life, will become easier with experience. It may not be perfect, so just do what seems best at the time.

What do you have to sell?

This might seem a strange question to ask at the beginning of an application process. Most students and recent graduates do not think of themselves as a product that they might have to 'sell' to an employer, but that is exactly how many employers view you. They want to 'buy' you in order for you to perform a role or offer a service in the most efficient and useful way possible for the benefit of the company, project or clients. Most will hope that whilst at work you will be happy, fulfilled and enjoy yourself, but their primary aim is likely to be financial. This is true whether you are applying for private or public sector companies. The private (sometimes called 'wealth creating') sector includes commercial radio, film and television, most print-based industry, production companies and creative arts, as much as the local sweet factory. Public sector includes mainly government-funded organisations such as schools, hospitals and social services. Of course the division between the two sectors is blurred, but both have finance at their heart. There is only so much money for an organisation to spend and when they 'buy' you as a member of staff or a product you are offering, they want to get good value for their money.

So if you think of yourself as a product that you want to sell, your application is like an advertisement – a way of getting someone to take notice of you. Imagine how you would struggle to develop an advert for a product without knowing what that product was. Trying to make applications without knowing what is your 'product', would be the same.

Filming in progress

So the first thing to consider is, what do you have to offer and who is going to be your customer?

It can be quite difficult to be objective and realistic about ourselves, so here are some ideas to get you started.

TIP

Write a sentence of about 50 words that summarises who you are, what you have done and what you can do. This can be a useful personal statement to introduce your CV.

Your sales point	Why employers might want it
Higher education	Having completed or studied at university level indicates to employers that you can think analytically, are independent and can learn. These are very important traits, whatever the subject or classification of your degree/diploma.
Being a graduate /diplomate	Many employers like the idea of employing someone who has studied for three years, passed exams, lived within an academic community and is educated.
Previous education	You are likely to have studied before entering higher education and have therefore developed other abilities and knowledge that might be useful to the employer.
Work experience	This tells the employer that someone else has seen fit to employ you and that again you have probably developed some useful skills.
IT	IT is now such an important part of most business, creative and commercial activity that without good IT skills you may have problems accessing jobs.
Personality	Surprisingly important in the workplace, your personality and interpersonal skills will be highly influential to potential employers.
Commitment	Employers are looking for people who really want to work – if you can put this enthusiasm across in applications you are halfway there.
Sports	Team activities are popular because employers like the idea you can lead or work well with others. They may also assume you are healthy (and be less likely to take sick leave).

Your sales point	Why employers might want it
Interests, hobbies	Employers do not always see the relevance of these to work, but if you are clever you can sell them as evidence of organisational skill, teamwork, dedication or many other desirable qualities
Youth/age	Whether you are a new fresh graduate, a mid-life career changer or a mature person, you can sell your age as an asset. If you are young, sell your adaptability and energy. If you are in mid-life, emphasise how hard you have worked to move into your new career, if you are mature, offer all that experience and expertise. Advertise positively.
Degree knowledge	For some posts this will be critical, but for many employers it's not the subject that matters but what you can do that counts.

Other people may be able to help you assess yourself and give you feedback about your strengths (and weaknesses if you ask). Family members can be a bit biased, but friends, partners, siblings and colleagues may be able to give you very useful data. It takes a bit of courage to look at yourself as others perceive you, but this is exactly what you need to do. You may be surprised at what people say, and you should be prepared for negatives and well as positives.

TIP

Write a short 'advert' for your friend or partner and ask them to do the same for you.

Careers advisers are trained to help you to explore who you are and what you have to offer an employer. Most careers services run 'drop in' sessions where you can talk to an adviser and many offer longer consultations. Make the most of any access you can get to professional careers advice.

There are more detailed self-awareness and self-evaluation tools widely available, both in book form and on the Internet. These can help you to clarify who you are, what your strengths and skills are, and give you ideas about how to describe these to employers.

Getting the employer to buy

Once you are sure what it is you have to sell, start looking for your potential buyers, people who might be prepared to pay you for your time, expertise and skills. There may be hundreds of companies potentially interested in you or there may be just one individual. In either case, it's up to you to identify them and find out everything you can about them. Check the work experience chapter for ideas of where to find vacancies and refer to your careers service for detailed information, particularly local. Once you have a vacancy in which you are interested, the work really starts. Many people, including graduates, fail to get jobs because they do not research the job and/or the organisation for which they are applying. This is a cardinal error.

Research is fundamental

Researching the job might sound like a boring or optional task, but it actually makes the difference between success and failure in applications. Employers complain that students and graduates just do not understand what it is they are applying for. One shocked manager told us: 'I was in the middle of interviewing this graduate when he admitted he didn't actually know what we make in our company.' Another told of a student on work experience who, after a month, was surprised to hear there was a factory attached to the office where she worked.

Doing thorough research will make you stand out from the rest of the applicants. It will instantly impress the recruiter. It will show all the skills, qualities and aptitudes that are so important to recruiters. Best of all, it is easy. You have spent many years in education learning to do exactly this. Use all those research skills you used when you were given a project to undertake, an essay to produce, a report to write or dissertation to research. Use the same or similar resources, commit time to the task and be focussed. If you do this and, very importantly, can demonstrate that you have done this, you will win over employers from the outset.

What and how to research

Before making an application, make sure you look carefully at the job role and the organisation involved. Bigger organisations will send detailed job descriptions, personnel specifications and company briefings.

Although you must read this carefully, highlighting key information, you should not rely solely on what is provided. Employers will be pleasantly surprised if you dig deeper and find out more about them than what is obvious. You will be amazed how few people do this, how useful it will be in writing your applications and how much it will impress recruiters.

When applying to smaller and medium-sized organisations, you may have to do more work on your own and be more creative and resourceful in finding out about them. Conversely, the more difficult it is to find out information, the more worth it has because it appears that you have really put effort into the research – a great boost to your chances. Always visit a company if at all possible – there is nothing like experiencing the place in reality.

Use this check list to record the information you need before you apply:

- ☑ Name of company/organisation
- ☑ Names of known individuals/contacts
- ☑ Address
- ☑ Telephone number
- ☑ Fax number
- ☑ Website address
- ☑ Nature of business – what they do or what they make
- ☑ If there is a vacancy, what exactly it is
- ☑ The salary, benefits, conditions of employment
- ☑ The size of the organisation (people and turnover)
- ☑ Location – local, regional, national, global
- ☑ The mission statement or stated values of the company
- ☑ The purpose of the organisation
- ☑ The financial situation of the organisation and how is it funded
- ☑ Whether there is a training package for new workers

You may think of many other aspects to research depending on the nature of the company.

When researching larger companies, you can use relevant websites or read directories and careers information. But what if you are interested in a small organisation, perhaps in the public sector or even an individual and there is no published material about them? We explore this next.

Speculative approaches

Most people do not realise that it is perfectly acceptable to contact an individual or organisation directly when seeking an opportunity or responding to a vacancy. You can email or telephone with a courteous request for further information. Explain exactly why you are calling, say what you want to know, be specific, brief and very polite.

Avoid calling early in the morning, especially on Mondays when people are likely to be busy. When using email, ask someone to check your tone, spelling and grammar. Always introduce yourself crisply and confidently:

> 'My name is Rob Greenwood and I would like very much to ask some questions about working at Sherwood House before completing my application',
> or
> 'I am a graduate called Sharon Booth and I want to send my CV to the right person in the organisation.'

Try to identify the right person who can help:

> 'I wonder if Ms Hussar is available,'
> or
> Would it be possible to speak to someone in the Editing Department who could help me,'
> or
> 'Do you have a few minutes to answer my three questions?'

Secretaries, receptionists, administrators and other staff can be fantastic allies. Be respectful and courteous to them and ask their advice if you can't seem to get further:

> 'I appreciate that you are very busy but I would be most grateful if you could suggest any way I could find out when Mr Burgess will be available,'
> or
> 'Could you give me any tips on how to approach Miss Owen,'
> or
> 'I am really keen to work at the company, could you tell me what kinds of people or skills they most often need?'

When you do get through to someone, whether by telephone or email, be absolutely clear about what you want to say. You are sure to annoy someone who is busy if you get through and then forget to mention what you meant to ask or can't remember details. They may well be interested in finding out something about you, so have your CV ready and be prepared to answer any questions that get thrown at you.

It is acceptable to ask about any information from the checklist above or further details about any published vacancy such as hours of work, exact nature of duties, travel requirements, but *only if* you couldn't have found this out by research elsewhere. Some people go to great lengths to find out esoteric and detailed information, which can be impressive to recruiters and interviewers. Going the extra mile or three will be well worth it.

And remember, even if all you research doesn't pay off and you don't get the opportunity you are trying for, the enhanced knowledge and information that you will have gained will give you a better and broader understanding of the working world.

Preparing yourself for application

You may have stacks of research about jobs, companies and what is available out there, but this is only half the equation. You must have detailed data about yourself to hand as well. There is no point in knowing all about the 'buyer' (the employer) if you don't know about the 'product' (that's you).

This is the moment when you climb into the loft or sort through all those old papers from school and college. (If you are living away from home you will need to enlist help or visit for a weekend).

You will need:

- ☑ Examination information: the exact subject titles, the examination boards for each subject (usually shown on the certificate), your grades or results, the month and year you got the result.
- ☑ National insurance number
- ☑ Medical number (NHS card)
- ☑ Chronological list of any work experience, including voluntary, part-time and vacation, with name of employer, dates worked, exact job title and a sentence describing your main duties for each
- ☑ A list of your key employability skills (see Chapter 1)
- ☑ A record of two people who are willing to be your referees. One should be someone who knows your academic ability – head-teacher, head of year, tutor, lecturer, principal, sixth-form teacher. One should be someone who knows you at work – supervisor, manager, foreman, section head, owner. For each person you need their title (Mr, Ms, Dr, Prof.), full name, professional role, address including postcode, telephone number and email address.

It can take a while to amass all this information but it will save you enormous amounts of time and effort if you collect it all together before you begin to apply for jobs.

> **TIP**
>
> You must ask people if they are willing to provide references for you and keep them well informed of what you are doing. Send them a copy of your CV and let them know what you are applying for. Send copies of your applications and information about the posts so they can write relevant references for you.

Your career action plan

It is useful, though not absolutely vital, to have goals when you are planning your future life and career. You probably already have goals, but perhaps you have never written them down, talked about them or perhaps even acknowledged them.

This exercise is designed to help you to identify some real goals and make an action plan on the basis of those goals. The purpose is to get you faster and more confidently to where you want to be.

You may have come across the idea of 'SMART' goals. SMART stands for **S**pecific, **M**easurable, **A**chievable, **R**ealistic and **T**ime-framed:

Specific – answers the questions who? when? where? what?

Measurable – you must set your own criteria for measuring achievement of your goal. It answers questions such as how much, how many?

Achievable – you will want to work towards your goal step by step, growing in confidence until you reach your target.

Realistic – you must be prepared and able to achieve your goal. If you believe in it, you can achieve it.

Time-framed – you must set timings for achieving goals, otherwise there is a danger of 'drift'.

You might say your goal is, for example, 'to be a successful film director', but this is too vague to be useful. What do you mean by 'successful' and how would you know when you've achieved it? If you restate your goal with SMART criteria it might look more like this:

Checking equipment to get the best possible angle

'By the time I am 30 years old I will have directed five films of at least 30-minutes each and have them played to audiences of at least 1,000 people.'

Your career goals

List at least three goals relating to your life or career. At this stage they can be short- or long-term. They can be goals relating to study, salary, location, creative development, personal relationships, membership of professions, level of job, type of work or anything you wish. They might even be about the sort of car you would like to drive or the house you want to live in. Write them as they come into your head, then write them again with SMART criteria.

1. ....

SMART: ....

....

....

2. ....

SMART: ....

....

....

3. ....

SMART: ....

....

....

TIP

Did you have trouble thinking up goals? Maybe you are not yet ready to plan your future or maybe you do not like detailed planning. It doesn't matter as long as you understand the process.

Once you have recorded three (or more) goals, choose the one that is most important to you. The next stage is to break down the goal into mini-goals to make it more manageable.

Example

SMART goal is 'Two years after graduating I will work on the West coast of the USA for at least a year in a major media corporation earning at least £24,000.'

Mini goals are:

1. Before I graduate I will carry out detailed research into the kinds of work placements and jobs that are available in the USA.
2. I will ask my parents about a friend who emigrated to California a few years ago and make contact with him for advice.
3. I will search the Internet for sites that help people to get work in the USA.
4. I will visit the careers library and read relevant information and maybe book an interview.
5. I will visit the library and bookshops to see if there are any key books I could use.

6. I will take any extra courses or options that would enhance my skills in areas that are needed in my target industry.
7. In the year after I graduate I will apply to companies that have business in the USA and explore possible transfers.
8. In the second year after I graduate I will apply to all my target companies and get advice from professionals about how to make my move.

You will see that what looked like quite a big, difficult goal can actually be broken down into much smaller less intimidating steps. The secret of success is to keep your big goal in the front of your mind and keep working at the mini goals that will make it happen in practice.

Creating an action plan

The final part of the career action plan is to keep a record of what you are doing so that you can see your goals getting irresistibly nearer.

Example

Julia has graduated from her MA in Photography and is planning her career one step at a time. Her career goal is 'to obtain full-time, relevant work in photography or related field by Spring next year near enough for me to travel to from home.'

You can create an action plan format that is right for you and works for your style of learning and self-management. You might prefer a big poster on your bedroom wall or a neat workbook. You might use your computer or a mind map. However you decide to do it, action planning should be effective, individualised, encouraging – and even fun! You can post little coloured notes on your mirror to remind yourself every morning of your next mini goal.

Use the form on p. 95 as model to record your progress towards your SMART goal:

TIP

Plan a treat to give yourself every time you achieve one of your mini goals. It could be a night out, something to pamper yourself, a walk in the country – anything that you enjoy.

Mini goal	Why this goal?	What resources can help me?	Time frame	Completed? (✓)
I need to find out all the local companies taking on casual staff for the summer	I need to pay off my overdraft, get some money and get back into the world of work	Library has local directory - and it's on-line there too. Local telephone book, evening newspaper. Ask at job centre?	By end of July	
I want to know what opportunities there are long-term for Photographers within a 15-mile radius of home	I want a proper job but I don't mind research-ing and planning til the right thing comes up	The careers service, my old tutors at uni - and maybe college, the library, destina-tions and labour market informa-tion off the Internet, company sites?	Before Christmas	
Send off at least 10 speculative applica-tions with my new CV to likely organisa-tions	I want to see whether I am being realistic - I'll also follow up with a phone call to get con-tacts and advice	CV pack from careers library, career sites on the web, get Dr Mason to check my letter	During the Christmas holidays - and send out in January	

SMART goal: ....

Mini goals	Why this goal – what are the benefits to me?	What resources/ who can help me?	Time frame	Completed? (✓)

Notes for teachers

Introducing the variety of decision-making techniques and helping students to understand their decisions are valuable classroom activities in which students can support each other. Individuals need to be confident and clear about what they have to 'sell' and what employers want to 'buy'. Cold-calling and speculative applications can be very intimidating and not just to students, yet in the film and media world it is something they will probably need to master. A career action plan could introduce action planning techniques useful for project design, revision or other academic purposes.

- In pairs or threes, students explain how they have made a recent decision and explore differences and difficulties.
- Students could interview a relative, friend, colleague or other contact to find out how they made their career decision. Pool and explore results.
- Introduce some decision-making techniques from technical or professional cultures (for example, storyboarding).
- Students write a 50- or 100-word 'sales' advert for radio, television or newspaper summarising themselves and what they have to offer.
- Practice 'cold-calling' in threes, with each student taking turns to be caller, applicant and observer. Each should report back on how it felt, how it sounded and how it could be improved.
- Goal setting and action planning can successfully be covered as a whole-group activity with students working together to help each other.

SEVEN Applications – next steps

By the end of this chapter you will know more about:

- Creating a winning CV
- Writing covering letters
- Writing letters of application
- Completing online and paper application forms
- Interviews and self-presentation
- Further selection processes

This chapter is designed to offer sound advice to individuals applying for vacancies in the film, media and related sectors; however, much of the content applies equally to applications for any jobs, graduate or otherwise. It builds on all the previous chapters and relies on an understanding of issues raised in them. Our advice is derived from many years' experience of helping students and graduates to break into these competitive fields and learning from the many examples of those who have been successful.

Your curriculum vitae

It may be quite a while since you wrote a CV or you may have created one recently. Either way it is worth reviewing exactly what your CV is for and why it is important.

CV stands for 'curriculum vitae', which means something like 'a list or course of life'. Its purpose is to show clearly facts about you that are relevant to a potential employer. Having a standard document helps employers to compare and select people more quickly and easily. The clearer and more professional your CV is, the more likely employers are to read it. There is plenty of room for individual style, but there are some definite guidelines. The first guideline is what to avoid. Use the checklist on p. 98 to ensure you are not doing something that allows employers to reject your CV.

CVs – 10 things employers HATE

BLANDNESS

That means a standard format downloaded from a computer program or the Internet, or something dull and uninspired.

What employers think: 'Lazy, uncreative, not IT literate, can't be bothered to present themselves well.'

ERRORS

Spelling, English usage or grammar mistakes.

What employers think: 'Can't proofread, can't be bothered to check their work', or 'Can't communicate in English'. FATAL and will be filed in WPB (waste paper bin).

HYPERBOLE

'I have extensive experience of film-making.' You are 21, the reader may be in their fifties – how extensive do you think it is? 'My degree has given me a comprehensive knowledge of all aspects of radio production.' If you believe that, you haven't understood your subject. Be accurate about your level of competence.

VAGUENESS

'I did various jobs in the office.' Like what? Make coffee? Tarzanogram? Be specific!

RAMBLING

Long paragraphs belong in an essay or a letter to your Mother.

What employers think: 'I haven't time to read this lot, I'll read the succinct CV next on the pile.'

TOO LONG

Seven-page CV.

What employers think: 'Can't prioritise, can't summarise and has overblown idea of own importance.'

TOO BRIEF

Lots of white spaces and hardly any information.

What employers think: 'Hasn't considered how to best present themselves and/or hasn't done anything with their life.'

(Continued)

INTERESTS and HOBBIES INAPPROPRIATE OR OVERSTATED

Fine in moderation if your interests have developed relevant skills, aptitudes and experience. Most sports, clubs, creative or intellectual pursuits, community and social activities are acceptable. Pubs, nightclubbing and train-spotting should be omitted.

What employers think: 'They won't be in until 11 a.m. and then they'll be hung over.'

DEPENDING ON YOUR PAST

Three-quarters of a page given over to GCSEs. Being a register monitor in 5B. Doing a paper round when you were 13.

What employers think: 'Hasn't done anything in last five years except sit in library or bar.'

NO REFEREES

What employers think: 'You are a misfit and no one likes you.'

Your CV should be as individual and unique as your own fingerprint. That is why we do not advocate borrowing someone else's style or using a standard downloadable format, nor are we proposing examples for you to copy. This applies to companies who claim to be able to create your CV for you. *No one* can create your CV except you. It does require time, thought and effort though.

It goes without saying that spelling and grammar errors on your written documents are unforgivable. If you are not confident about this aspect, have a professional check it for you.

Getting started

Think about who is going to read your CV. Is it likely to be a personnel/human resources manager in a big corporation or a busy, self-employed creative person?

Consider the type of vacancy you are aiming for. Is it a professional, traditional, rather conventional position or an innovative, individual job with a funky organisation?

How do you want to present yourself? Are you a trend-aware, contemporary youthful enthusiast or a more dependable, steady, mature type?

Thinking about these things should give you some useful clues about how to present your CV. Every aspect, from the paper it is printed on, whether to add graphics or images, the font styles, the size of font, the layout, the vocabulary and tone you adopt, everything says something about you. And remember, the employer only has your CV and cover letter to look at; they can't see you, imagine what you are like or realise how wonderful you are. You have to make that CV work for you.

To make things a little more complicated, if you want to apply for work in creative and media fields, you may want to illustrate your creativity. Perhaps these examples will be inspirational:

- A final year graphics and journalism student was committed to working for a music magazine. He presented his CV as two pages from such a magazine, designed by himself and printed up in colour.
- A PR student was desperate to get into fashion promotion. She created a little pocket book that was her CV and also showcased her best work. It was printed in full colour on card and looked very professional.
- A design student made his CV into a tea packet and put his information on little tea bags to be pulled out and read.
- A web and multimedia graduate created a web CV and simply sent out the address on a compliment slip he had designed.

You do not have to do anything like this if it doesn't feel right for the job you are applying for, but the examples above illustrate how important it is that your CV truly reflects the best of you and sells it effectively to the employer.

It is much better practice to send five fantastic, perfect CVs out to five targeted employers than sending a hundred mediocre ones to any old companies in the desperate hope that someone will respond. The first five will all be in the top of the pile. The hundred will all be at the bottom of the piles.

> **TIP**
>
> Targeting your CV is critical to success. Mention the specific vacancy and organisation by name. Link everything to the job and the company. The reader will then feel you are applying to them, not just sending a standard CV.

Your CV will need constant updating, so it is a work in progress. Use the checklist on pp. 101–2 to make sure you are hitting most of the right things.

CV CHECKLIST	Comment or ✓
Presentation	
Initial impact – does this CV look good? Is it attractive? Hold it at arm's length and see if it has visual impact.	
Is it well balanced across the two pages, with sections logically presented on the page?	
Are the fonts used appropriate, easy to read and visually interesting?	
What about layout? If you were an employer, could you tell immediately where to find any information about this applicant or is it confusing?	
Content	
Check carefully – can you spot any errors or mistakes at all?	
Is there a career objective or personal profile? If there is, is it targeted clearly at the employer and/or vacancy?	
Is your name, address, telephone number, mobile and email easily spotted?	
Looking at it with employer's eyes, are the really interesting, exciting and relevant details on the first page?	
Looking at the degree, is it clear what has been studied, which modules are most relevant to the job and which you liked most?	
Is the expected degree classification mentioned?	
Is the subject of the degree clear and well presented?	
Is the dissertation subject mentioned?	
Can you quickly scan the back-up qualifications, that is, those taken before the degree?	

CV CHECKLIST	Comment or ✓
Work experience – is the most relevant experience mentioned first and in most detail?	
Work experience – is it clear who was the employer, what was the role, what skills were gained and when you were there?	
Is there a skills profile, clearly describing the employability skills you have?	
If there is a hobbies/interests section, is it relevant to the vacancy and does it add positive information about you?	
What about other sections – is it clear why they are included and do they add to the CV or just fill space?	
Is the tone of the CV correct – not too informal but with some personality?	

And remember to keep your CV up to date and to let your referees have revised copies regularly.

Covering letters

This guidance also applies to a covering email if you are sending your CV electronically, as is often the case now.

Sending a covering letter or email is a courtesy. It introduces your CV to the reader and acts as a bridge, clearly showing the relationship between the vacancy or desired post and the information on the CV. There is a correct layout and standard style for business letters and it is up to you to make the best version of this. A cover letter should be no longer than one side of A4 (about 300 words). It should echo the CV in all regards. It should be presented on the same kind of paper, using the same printer and font. In other words, make sure the two documents belong together. If you are using images or graphics, perhaps you can show a lighter version on the letter. Avoid making it look as if the letter or email is an afterthought.

You should use a standard business letter layout with your own address and telephone number at the top. This can be to the right, centred or, increasingly often, left aligned. You must include the date, addressee's details, and then the correct salutation: 'Dear Mr/Mrs/Miss/Ms/Dr Bloggs'. Where you aren't sure which title is correct you can adopt the modern style 'Dear Robin Bloggs'. You should end with 'Yours sincerely.' Try to aviod 'Dear Sir/Madam', but if you have to, you must match it with 'Yours faithfully'. Don't forget to sign it.

Make sure that the letter is sensibly spread over the page. If it seems short or cramped, bring the margins in, and make sure there is a clear space between the paragraphs. If it still looks 'lost' on the page, try going up a font size.

Leave a space after commas, full stops, colons, and semicolons.

Decide whether you want to use a standard font like Times New Roman, or a sans serif font like Arial, or another font of your own choice. How conventional do you want to appear? Are they looking for creativity? Will the font from your home computer print out on the university system? Use the same font as you use for your CV.

TIP
If you are emailing your CV and letter, the formatting is likely to be lost, so have a simple version with the same content but no graphics or formatting to send instead.

Use the checklist on p. 104 to make sure your cover letter does you and your CV justice.

Try to emphasise what *you* can offer the company, not what they can do for you. Remember that you are a 'product' and you want them to 'buy'.

TIP
There are loads of examples of CVs and cover letters on the web and in careers libraries – don't copy them, but you can use them for inspiration if you run out of ideas.

Letters of application

This section applies to all those occasions when you have to produce an extended piece of writing about yourself in response to an employer's request. It could be something in a vacancy advertisement like:

'Write a letter explaining why we should employ you.'
'Send a letter of application to ... '
'Please apply in writing to ... '

COVER LETTER CHECKLIST	Comment or ✓
Presentation	
Does your covering letter look attractive and make you want to read it? Ask someone to check it for you.	
Is it presented well on the paper with not too much white space and the content evenly balanced on the pages?	
Is the font appropriate in style and size? And not too many font styles?	
Does it look and feel as if it is related to your CV?	
Is it correctly laid out in a business style?	
Content	
Is your address, telephone number and email clearly shown?	
Is the employer's name and company shown?	
Is there an appropriate reference line to tell the employer what the letter is about?	
Is the salutation correct and does it use a person's name?	
Is your opening paragraph interesting and does it tell the employer exactly why you are writing?	
Does the main part of the letter tell the employer relevant information about your study, work experience and skills and how these relate to the vacancy? Does it make you want to read the CV?	
Is the closing paragraph a polite sign-off and does it clearly indicate what happens next?	
Tone – is the letter formal, polite but with personality?	
Is the letter correctly signed off and is your name printed below the signature?	

Or it might be within an application form; sometimes there are large spaces with a very general guide question for you to use to apply to the job. Or you may want to write a longer letter in a speculative application. If it is a letter, follow the business style guidelines as for the covering letter.

You are advised to approach all these in a logical and methodical manner. Don't just start writing and hope something good will emerge.

The first thing to do is go back to the job description, personnel specification and further particulars for the post. If these documents are not available, you will have to use general careers information or vacancies to find relevant job descriptions. Make sure you have done all possible research as described in the work experience chapter. Check that you have your up-to-date personal details to hand, too.

Length

You will need to write atleast one side of A4, (that is at least 500 words) to be credible. That might sound a lot, but many people find themselves writing more than this.

Presentation

Always word process if possible. Spell check but also have someone check it for you before sending, as spell checking will not show words that are correct but out of context (for example 'their' instead of 'there'). Keep font size and style easy to read.

Tone

You should write in a formal manner in full sentences and in the first person singular. Keep sentences brief and clear and make each and every one say something positive.

Content

It is perfectly acceptable to break the piece into sub-headed sections. There are various ways of doing this. For example, you could refer to the job description and use each requirement as a sub-heading, explaining how you meet the criteria. Or you could refer to your CV and sub-head each aspect of your education, work experience and skills, illustrating how they match the job requirements. You might decide your own preferred way of sub-heading and organising the long application. In any case, think about and plan what you want to say in each sub section. It's fine for there to be only one or two sentences in each because employers will find the pertinent information more quickly

quickly and easily, which will create a positive impression of your organisation and communication skills.

Top and tail

It is important to make a strong impact with your first and last sentences. A conventional way to open is something like: 'I wish to be considered for the post of XXXX and offer the following information in support of my application.' If you are confident you can pull it off, you could try something more dynamic and cheeky such as: 'When I read your vacancy I knew I would be a perfect candidate for this role.'

To finish effectively, summarise what you have written, again linking strongly to the post or vacancy.

TIP

Keep a copy of your long application or letter as you will need to read it through before your interview.

Completing online and paper application forms

Most of you will be very familiar with using the Internet and email to communicate. Keep in mind all the previous advice about applications and you won't go far wrong.

Online job applications can be deceptive because you fill in boxes, click to send them and they arrive instantaneously, so it can be tempting to treat them casually. In fact, they need just as much preparation and thought as conventional paper applications. Never use shortened text-style abbreviations such as '2nite' for 'tonight'. Keep your tone and approach formal. Take as much time preparing for your e-application as you would for a paper-based one. To begin, download or copy the form, think about the questions and prepare draft answers.

There are advantages to online applications. They can be quicker to complete as you can use pull-down lists for repeat details, for example, exam subjects, grades and so on.

A big advantage is that you can cut and paste answers from Word documents, of course checking your spelling and grammar as you go. Do this off-line as many employers will omit spell and grammar checks deliberately.

Be prepared

When you start an online application you may be surprised to find yourself diverted to a test centre to conduct an online numeracy or literacy test. You may wish to defer the test so that you can go and prepare a bit before you take it. Sometimes tests will reject you from the recruitment process and you won't be able to continue the online application (this sometimes happens when you put A-level grades in too).

You get faster responses and decisions from employers when applying online and it can be quite a shock to get an email response minutes after you have sent a form electronically.

Most employers insist that all forms are seen by real people, so you won't be selected or rejected by a computer.

Answering questions

These guideline are relevant to both paper-based and online applications.

1. Answer the question, remembering that employers are looking for skills and evidence of those skills from your experience. Sell yourself to employers by giving evidence from as many parts of your life as possible, including work experience, part-time jobs, sports, community activities, social life and so on to help you to match the employer's requirements.
2. Some questions are really two or even three or more questions. These multi-part questions require an answer for each part. A typical one might be: 'Describe a time when you had to overcome a problem, what was the problem, what did you do, and what was the outcome.' Use separate paragraphs, ideally with short subheadings. It helps you and the selector to know that you have answered all parts of the question.
3. Keep answers brief and to the point, but with enough information to convince the reader. Show your draft to a careers adviser, family member, tutor or, even better, someone working in the field you are hoping to enter.
4. Never leave an answer blank. They are there for a reason and it irritates employers if you don't try to answer. If something really does not apply to you, then you should write N/A to show you have seen the question and not just missed it out. Some online systems won't let you proceed to the next question until you have answered the previous one.

Finally

It is well worth finding someone to check your application before you push the 'send' button, not only for spelling and grammar mistakes, but also to check if you have made a good job of selling yourself. Anything between 60 per cent and 90 per cent of applications are rejected at the application stage, so prepare well to make sure you are not one of them.

TIP

Careers libraries have lots of useful booklets and DVDs related to applications and online applications. You can save yourself a lot of wasted time by visiting them and carefully reading or viewing their resources.

Interviews and self-presentation

How do you feel about attending a selection interview? Nervous? Excited? Worried that you'll do or say something stupid? Few of us are immune to the terror of interviews and it is perfectly normal for the adrenaline to be flowing. Coping with nerves is a personal thing, but students have suggested the following to help:

- Do lots of preparation because the more you know about the job, the fewer chances there are that you'll be caught out.
- Take five deep breaths before going in the room and occasionally take some deep breaths whilst you are in the interview.
- Plan the journey so you will arrive well before and have time to chill out with a stroll or cup of tea.
- Wear something in which you feel comfortable and smart, not necessarily a brand new suit or pair of shoes.
- Don't overuse make-up, perfume or aftershave and make sure hair is tidy.
- Imagine the panel are naked or in another undignified position so that you don't feel scared of them.
- They are people too and will respond to a warm smile and enthusiasm.

Remember, if you are invited to an interview, it means your application was successful and the company (or course leader) is interested in meeting you. That in itself means you've done something right; it is an expensive business to interview candidates and employers don't waste time on people they aren't seriously considering. So everything is going well for you so far.

Preparing for your interview

Check the details

When you receive the invitation, whether by post or telephone, make sure you check as many details as possible:

- Where do you have to go for the interview?
- When do you have to be there?
- Who will be interviewing you?
- Do you have to take any documents?
- Are there any special instructions, such as presentations you should prepare?

First impressions are really important. If a handshake seems appropriate, try for a firm (but not crushing), dry handshake and look the interviewer in the eye when you shake hands, making good eye contact and smile warmly. Wait to be asked to be seated (or if they fail to invite you, say 'Shall I sit here?').

Read all the information sent

It will help you to know the likely structure of the interview and what to expect. If this information is not in the invitation, call the employer or course leader and ask. Be polite and have specific questions. They may not always be keen to give you details, but that in itself is quite informative.

One student arrived for an interview and discovered she was expected to give a 10-minute presentation. She had been told this on a separate sheet in the interview pack, but hadn't read it.

Arrange the day

You may need to negotiate time off from work or study. It is nearly always advisable to be honest about why you need the time. Check travel times. Aim to arrive with an hour in hand. Make sure you know exactly where you are expected to arrive – some companies and campuses are very large. You may need to consider an overnight stay. If you have no contacts in the area, check with the personnel or student advice office for suggestions for budget accommodation. The nearest YMCA, YWCA or a backpacker's hostel may be able to help.

Research and read

Read your application and highlight aspects you might be asked about. Arrange for someone to ask you questions based on your application – you might get some surprises.

You may be able to arrange a practice interview. Ask at your careers service initially, otherwise a friend or colleague may be able to help. You will need to do some even more detailed research on the organisation or course if at all possible, so check Chapter 5 on work experience for suggestions.

Types of interview

One-to-one

Just one person interviewing you.

- You will need to make a good relationship and respond positively to make a strong impression.

Panel

You are much more likely to experience this as it is recommended from an equal opportunities aspect. The panel can consist of anything between two and seven members; three or four is recommended and most common.

- Each individual will ask you questions in turn. Reply to the person who has asked the question, but respond to the whole panel by glancing at them from time to time when answering.

Carousel

'Mini' interviews with a number of individuals; perhaps you will move from one office to the next.

- You will need to be quick on your toes and able to adapt to different people very flexibly. Try to think about the different perspectives each individual will have.

Presentation

Many interviews include a presentation, which you will normally be told about beforehand.

- Make sure you know the timing and subject required.
- Check the venue before if possible.
- Prepare hand-outs in advance.

- You will usually be given details of PowerPoint or other audio-visual equipment to be used.
- Make sure your presentation is well structured and relevant.
- Speak clearly, pace yourself and do not read from notes directly.
- *Practice* beforehand, in front of an audience if possible.

Audition

Depending on the field or performance, you will be briefed on the length and nature of your audition. Before attending, seek guidance from relevant, experienced professionals. Practice, practice, practice. Before, during and after the audition maintain a polite and calm demeanour. You are being assessed on your personality as much as your technical skills.

Formal/informal

Never forget, social events, lunches and tours are part of the interview. There is no such thing as an 'informal' interview.

You may experience any combination of the above.

What to expect

In a professional, well-conducted interview you should experience the following:

- Questions will be carefully designed to elicit information.
- You will be given plenty of opportunity to speak.
- You will be able to ask questions.
- It will feel like a two-way discourse, challenging but not uncomfortable.
- The interviewer will ask questions relevant to the post.
- They will often be looking for evidence to fit pre-set criteria.
- You will be able to get feedback afterwards.

It is relatively easy to prepare answers for a professional interview. You can predict what will be covered. Criterion-led interviewing means that the process of interviewing is as fair as possible; 'the best person for the job'.

In an amateur, poorly conducted interview you may experience the following. It may be that the interviewer, whilst great at their job, has no training in interviewing and they may be as nervous as you are:

- Questions may be haphazard – you will have to manage the process.
- You may not get the opportunity to speak.
- There may be little opportunity to ask questions.
- You may be asked questions which make you uncomfortable or are illegal.
- The interviewer may be poorly prepared, with no clear structure or theme.
- There may be little feedback afterwards.

These interviews are much more difficult to manage. You will have to be proactive and ensure that you say what you need to, despite what the interviewer does.

TIP

If you have managed to get an interview through a speculative application (well done), you will have to actively manage the interview by strongly and imaginatively selling your skills and what you can offer the company.

Interview questions

The good news is, there are only three kinds of questions that can be asked at interview: closed, open and hypothetical.

Closed questions

These only really require a one-word answer:

> 'Did you do well in Maths?'
> 'Have you read our brochure?'
> 'Were you the captain of any sports team?'

But closed questions can make for a very tedious interview. If your interviewer asks closed questions, you might turn them into more open ones:

> 'Have you any experience of pin-ball machine design?'

Don't answer 'No' or even 'Yes'. Try 'I have never actually designed one of these machines, but I did design a roller-ball machine, very similar in many ways to pin-ball structure.'

You can nearly always use this 'Yes ... but' technique to turn the question around to something you want to tell the interviewer.

However, don't be afraid to give one word answers now and then ... 'Do you want the job?'

Open questions

The answer usually requires more than one word:

'What did you most enjoy about study?'
'What do you think about the current crisis?'
'What experiences most influenced your career choice?'
'Tell me about yourself.'

These are easier to cope with, but beware of over-answering, especially when nervous.

If you are asked an open question, you might want to limit the answer yourself:

'What do you want to achieve?'
Response:
'In the next three years I would like to ...'

Judge how much the interviewer wants you to respond from her reactions. You can always check by saying:

'Is that sufficient information?'
or
'Would you like me to continue?'

Hypothetical questions

These type of questions ask for a fantasy answer:

'If you had your time over again, what would you study?'
'Imagine you are marketing manager for Pedicat Petfood. A pressure group claims that there is whale meat in the product and there is a public outcry. What would you do?'
'If you were given this job, what would be the main areas of development you would wish to pursue?'

TIP

Do not rush to answer hypothetical questions. Take your time and ask for a few seconds to consider if necessary. Your first ideas may be improved by a few seconds reflection and it will look like you've thought about it.

Remember, a hypothetical question will receive a hypothetical answer. What is the interviewer looking for?

- It may be the ability to think creatively and on your feet.
- It may be logic and reasoned argument, justifying what you decide.
- It may be technical knowledge or understanding.
- They may not even know themselves.

In any case, think carefully and objectively before you start to answer – these can be the trickiest questions of all.

TIP

A competent interviewer will base the interview on open questions and make selective use of closed and hypothetical questions.

Typical interview questions

There are typical questions that many interviewers will ask. You may find it useful to practice answering these:

'Why did you apply to study at your chosen university?'
'Why did you apply for the course you are studying?'
'Tell me about your course.'
'Which part of your course did you enjoy/dislike most, and why?'
'What was your dissertation/special option topic and why did you choose it?'
'Why did you do a degree/HND?'
'What did you enjoy most at school?'
'What positions of responsibility have you held at school/college/university?'
'What benefits have you gained from work experience? (This can be interpreted as any work experience)'.
'Why have you chosen this company/profession?'
'What do you know about this company/profession?'
'What do you understand by, for example, personnel, financial management and so on?'
'What are your ambitions?'
'What do you hope to be doing five years from now?'

'What skills do you think are needed for this position?'
'Tell me about your interests, hobbies, extracurricular activities.'
'What has been your greatest challenge in life, and how did you overcome it?'
'What is your greatest strength?'
'What is your greatest weakness?'
'Why do you want to work for this particular company/study this particular course?'
'How do you cope under stress?'
'How would your friends (or family or work colleagues) describe you?'
'How would you describe yourself?'
'What newspapers do you read, and why?'
'What are your short-, medium- or long-term ambitions?'
'Are you ambitious?'
'How do you react to criticism?'
'What do you dislike doing?'
'Give me an example of something that happened to you – what went wrong, how did you cope?'
'Give me an example of something you have done that was successful – what obstacles did you have to overcome and how did you do it?'
'How do you prioritise?'
'How would you deal with aggressive customers or clients?'
'Why should we appoint you?'

After the interview

Think about the interview but don't dwell morbidly on it. Think about any questions you could have answered better or that you were unprepared for.

Success

- If you have been successful, you will be informed formally by letter.
- Check out all details of the post and ensure that all is well.
- Sometimes, your appointment will be subject to medical clearance or references.
- You might enquire about relocation expenses or financial help in your first weeks.
- Write formally to accept the job, under the stated conditions, if these are acceptable.
- Getting the job is only the start – you have lots to learn in your new career.

Failure

- If you haven't got the job, don't worry – it probably wasn't right for you.
- At the very least it was good experience – what have you learnt from it?
- You can often get feedback on your performance – contact the people who interviewed you.
- Keep trying and don't give up.
- To get the interview was an achievement in itself.

---

10 top tips for interviews

1. Dress to feel confident, comfortable and able to be yourself.
2. Get to bed early for two or three nights before the interview date – you probably won't sleep well the night before.
3. Be polite and pleasant to everyone you meet on the day – and you *can* smile at people.
4. Practice your handshake and eye contact before you attend for interview.
5. Check your sitting posture in a mirror – do you look alert without looking nervous?
6. Do sufficient preparation so you feel confident about what you are applying for – but there's no need to over-cram.
7. Prepare two or three questions and write them in a notebook – its easy to forget them.
8. Treat the first two or more interviews as practice. Learn all you can and get feedback.
9. Keep a record of all your interviews and notes on how they went.
10. Think positive – you have lots to offer – and be yourself.

Further selection processes

We want to mention that there may be other forms of selection that you come across. If you feel at all uncertain about any aspect of selection, we encourage you to get further guidance and advice from careers professionals who are very experienced in the different methods that employers use. Here are a few examples to be aware of:

- **Discussions and debates**: You may be asked to take part in a formalised role play, debate or discussion with others. Recruiters are looking for communication and team skills as well as the ability to maintain your own position yet give a fair hearing to others. Topics can be anything employers choose but are often aspects of the job you are applying to, current events or news stories, a business dilemma or issue. There is not necessarily a right or wrong outcome for these debates; the recruiters are more interested in how you handle the information and yourself during the process. Keep a careful eye on timing as this often creates problems in group discussions.
- **Giving a presentation either in group or alone**: It is very common now to be asked to prepare a presentation as part of the recruitment process. The topic may be stated by the recruiter or they may ask you to speak on your own choice of topic. In either case you will be given a strict time limit. Speak clearly and at a good pace, use audio-visual aids if at all possible, maintain eye contact and a relationship with the audience and prepare yourself for probing questions.
- **In-tray exercise**: You may be given a pile of documents (electronic or hard copy) and asked to sort out and respond to the conflicting issues within them. There is never enough time to do this justice, so think carefully about your (and the organisation's) priorities and be prepared to justify any decisions you have made.
- **Group/team activity (indoor or outdoor)**: This involves being asked to perform some unusual or challenging task in a group and is designed to test for organisational skill, creativity, leadership and so on. Do your best, join in with whatever the activity is, and focus on the process as much as the task. How you get things done is just as important as getting them done.
- **Psychometric testing**: There are two main kinds of psychometric tests that you may come across. There are *personality tests*, which usually consist of a series of forced-choice questions, and *ability tests*, which can cover a range of skills (verbal, numerical or spatial) and may be forced or multiple choice. Either may be completed electronically or by pen and paper. Either may be included in online application processes. You can take practice tests online or in your careers service and this can be quite useful to do anyway, even if you don't expect to take recruitment tests. There are techniques that will help you cope with psychometrics, and detailed guidance is best given by a professional careers adviser.

Notes for teachers

Students often focus on their applications and interview techniques. Encouraging them to work through previous exercises, such as auditing their employability skills, should greatly improve their CVs and ability to cope with the selection process. There are hundreds of activities which can enhance their career management and application skills.

- In pairs, critique example CVs and make a list of good and bad points. Present these to rest of group.
- Take example application form questions and create model answers in pairs or teams.
- Create application packs with a vacancy and jobs details and four CVs to match against the criteria – which is best, and why?
- Practice interview in triads with each participant taking turns to be interviewer, interviewee and observer.
- Practice presentations of different lengths and with different approaches and topics.

Final words

If you have read through all the chapters in Part I and undertaken the exercises and tips we have suggested, you will have put yourself in a very good position to succeed in your life and career. But of course, things very seldom turn out exactly as we plan or expect. Be ready to take opportunities that come unexpectedly. Be flexible, optimistic and positive in all you do. Career planning is as much an instinctive process as a logical one, and sometimes you may just 'feel' something is right.

Part II of this book offers a comprehensive vision of some of the many different career options available to you, seen through the eyes of real people involved in film and media.

'Keep interested in your own career, however humble: it is a real possession in the changing fortunes of time.'

M. Ehrmann, *Desiderata*, 1927

Appendix: resources library

The following resources will help you in exploring many aspects of careers information and advice.

General websites

URL	What's there?
www.postgrad.hobsons.com	*Hobsons Postgraduate Directory.*
www.prospects.ac.uk	Contains much of the information available in the *Prospects Postgraduate Directory.*
www.grantfinder.co.uk	*GrantFinder.*
www.artifact.ac.uk	A guide to Internet resources in the arts and creative industries.
www.arts-connect.net	Search engine dedicated to the arts.
www.csv.org.uk	CSV is a social action broadcaster that offers media training to a variety of client groups.
www.culture.gov.uk	Department of Culture, Media and Sport; information and advice on sources of funding.
www.prospects.ac.uk	Graduate Prospects is the national graduate careers website and offers a full range of occupational information, guidance, vacancies, interviews and application advice, postgraduate courses, careers fairs and much more.
www.ideasfactory.com	The Ideas Factory gives support to new entrants to creative industries.

www.mediabridge.org.uk	Mediabridge, published by CSV, is a regular e-newsletter, highlighting opportunities for media training, jobs and work experience across the UK.
www.mediauk.com	This is an independent media employer directory for the UK. Contains news and job vacancies.
www.mediauk.com	Careers information, case studies and links to other sources.

Recommended reading

Hobsons Graduate Career Directory (2004). Richmond, Surrey: Trotman & Co Ltd.

Prospects Postgraduate Directory (annual). Manchester: HECSU.

Copies can be purchased direct from the publisher and are also available in career libraries. Much of the information is also now online (see url above).

Smythe et al. (2003) *Directory of Grant Making Trust*. Tonbridge, Kent: Charities Aid Foundation.

Prospects Postgraduate Funding Guide (annual). Manchester: HECSU.

Copies can be purchased direct from the publisher and are also available in career libraries.

Jenner, S. (2000) *The Graduate Career Handbook*, Financial Times. Englewood Cliffs, NJ: Pearson Educational.

This is an excellent all-round guide to applying for your first job and takes you through the first months of graduate work.

Llewellyn, S. (2003) *A Career Handbook for TV, Radio, Film, Video and Interactive Media*. London: Skillset.

A useful guide, though not aimed specifically at graduates.

Alden, C. (2004) *On Air: The Guardian Guide to a Career in TV and Radio*. London: Guardian Books.

Written by media journalists with contributions from top writers and presenters.

Eikelberry, C. (1999) *The Career Guide for Creative and Unconventional People*. Berkeley, CA: Ten Speed Press.

US based but very encouraging reading for the more creative student or graduate

The following resources are referred to in the text, and are presented roughly in the order in the which they appear.

Introduction

Gregory, G. (1999) 'Career Aspirations of Students of Film and Media at Five UK Universities', MA Cultural Studies. Unpublished MA Thesis, University of Lincolnshire and Humberside.

Skillset (2003) *A Bigger Future: The UK Film Skills Strategy*. London: Skillset.

Chapter 1

AGCAS (Association of Graduate Careers Advisory Services) (2001): www.agcas.org.uk

Skillset (2002) *Working Freelance*. London: Skillset.

Skillset Careers Advice: www.skillset.org/careers

Lifelong Learning Career Development Loans: www.lifelonglearning.co.uk/cdl

Unofficial guides to UK universities: www.unofficial-guides.com

Job Profiles: www.skillset.org/careers/jobs/

Skillset Workforce Survey (2004): www.skillset.org/interactive

UK Film Council (2003) Statistical Yearbook: www.ukfilmcouncil.org.uk/

Universities and Colleges Admissions Service (UCAS): www.ucas.com

UK Trade and Investment (2005) *Export Services Guide for the TV Industries*. London: UK Trade and Investment.

Skillset (2002) *Employment Census of Audio Visual Industries*. London: Skillset.

UK Film Council (2003): http://www.ukfilmcouncil.org.uk/

The British Film Institute (BFI): www.bfi.org.uk/

The Commercial Radio Companies Association: www.crcd.co.uk

IVCA (International Visual Communications Association): www.ivca. org/

Graduate Prospects – Destinations: www.prospects.ac.uk

Jenkins, M. (2003) *Creative Careers: Film*. Richmond: Trotman and Channel 4 Ideas.

Prospects Postgraduate Directory (annual). Manchester: HECSU.

Smythe et al. (2003) *Directory of Grant Making Trust*. Tonbridge, Kent: Charities Aid Foundation.

Prospects Postgraduate Funding Guide (annual). Manchester: HECSU.

Chapter 2

Skillset (2004) *Skillset Census Results 2004*, www.skillset.org

AGCAS Sector Briefings: Creative and Cultural, 2005: www.agcas.org.uk

Higher Education Careers Service Unit (HECSU): www.hecsu.ac.uk

Morrison, I. (2004) www.skillset.org/skillset/press/2004/article_2980_1.asp

Samuelson, M. (2006) Skillset Event, 'Careering into the AV Industries', 21 March, Commonwealth Club, London.

Pearman, I. (2005) *Is Anyone Listening?* London: Creative and Cultural Skills Council.

ADI: www.theadigroup.com/

Dragon's Garden: www.dragons-garden.co.uk/

Shooting People: www.shootingpeople.org

Talent Circle: www.talentcircle.co.uk

Prospects Directory Salary and Vacancy Survey: www.prospects. ac.uk/cms/

Jenkins, M. (2003) *Creative Careers: Film*. Richmond: Trotman and Channel 4 Ideas.

Chapter 4

myspace: www.myspace.com/

Goffman, E. (1956) *The Presentation of Self in Everyday Life*. New York: Doubleday.

Goldman, E. (2004) *As Others See Us : Body Movement and the Art of Successful Communication*, New York: Routledge.

Chapter 5

UK National Volunteering Organisation: www.do-it.org.uk

UK Health and Safety Executive: www.hse.gov.uk/

Pearman, I., cited above.

Chapter 6

Graduate national vacancies in film, media, broadcast and creative media: www.prospects.ac.uk

A comprehensive list of vacancy sites is available through the prospects website cited above. Check under Contacts and Resources: www.prospects.ac.uk/cms/

Applications, CVs, interviews: www.prospects.ac.uk/cms/ShowPage/ Home_page/Applications__CVs_and_interviews/pleefmd

Chapter 7

Applications, CVs, Interviews: www.prospects.ac.uk/cms/ShowPage/ Home_page/Applications__CVs_and_interviews/p!eefmd

Chapter 8

Skillset (2005) *Survey of the Audio Industries' Workforce 2005:* www. skillset.org/research/article_5113_1.asp

Gibson, J. (ed.) (2007) *Guardian Media Directory 2007: The Essential Handbook*. London: Guardian Newspapers Ltd.

PART II

Road to the real world: insiders' advice on careers in the media

Welcome to Part II of *Careers in Media and Film*. Here you can explore a number of career opportunities in the media, particularly the ones most popular with students and graduates, including film, television, radio, newspaper and magazine journalism, publishing and multimedia. The chapters that follow have been written exclusively and specifically for this book by professionals in the field who know what it is like to start at the bottom and who offer real-life examples of how to get into these competitive industries.

These experts explore issues such as what the sectors are like, what roles are available, which qualifications you will need for different roles, how to learn about particular job opportunities, how to get the first job and how to advance your career. They identify the most important skills needed in a particular media industry and explain what is involved in performing various roles. In addition, they discuss the job market, working conditions, financial and other rewards of working in the various sectors of the industry.

The authors of the chapters are themselves practitioners who have first-hand experience of working in the respective industries, and many of them combine employment in the media with academic work. To enrich this perspective, you will also find interviews with graduates and others working in the industry.

These case studies will give you realistic illustrations of career experiences in film and media – both the good and the not-so-good aspects. Informative and accessible, these chapters are a must-read for anybody who dreams about becoming a success in the media.

Remember, even if you are not interested in the exact roles described in this section, the lessons and information you will gain are transferable and relevant to a wide range of careers in the industry.

If you want to find out more about a particular industry, occupation or aspect of the career, there are references to further resources at the end of each of the chapters.

Notes for teachers

Here are some ideas for using this material for personal development planning (PDP), employability skills development and career management activities and exercises.

- Students analyse the content of a chapter, identifying the skills required to carry out the role effectively. They then match their employability skills (Chapter 3) to those identified.
- Students explore problems and issues around how the case study examples successfully enter the various careers. They can identify successful strategies for entry into employment and how they could implement these within their own careers management. What skills will they need to acquire in order to do this?
- These case studies can be used as a template for students to carry out an exercise whereby they interview a practitioner and produce a similar piece of writing to share with the class and for their own personal use. This would extend the knowledge base for the whole class, enabling students to cover alternative careers.
- A similar exercise can be to take one (most relevant) case study and ask students or groups of students to explore other jobs within the sector, for example, in journalism or radio there are numerous different roles that may be of interest.
- Take two practitioners in a similar job or within an industry and compare and contrast the experiences of both, perhaps using one of the case studies as a starting point.

EIGHT Film-making

Film industry overview

The film business is of course global and multinational. You might immediately think of Hollywood and Bollywood, but there is also a strong and developing industry in the UK. At present this UK industry is mainly limited to the southeast of England, but there are signs that this is going to change as the regions are beginning to invest in film projects.

This means there are lots of exciting opportunities, and it can seem immensely attractive to students and graduates, especially those with a real passion for films and film-making. There is a huge range of careers within the film industry but, it must be said, it is notoriously difficult to break into. However, there are ways and means of getting in and a dedicated student or graduate, from whatever discipline, should not be deterred from exploring possible entry routes.

Careers in the film industry

Anyone who has sat through the credits at the end of a blockbuster, which sometimes seem to be as long as the film itself, will know that film-making, like other media careers, embraces a very diverse range of occupations. These can be categorised in a variety of ways.

On the creative side there is writing, editing, directing, acting, costume, set design, computer-aided design (CAD), animation, prop- and model-making, graphics and specialist creative roles. Then there are the technical roles such as lighting, electrical, camera work, sound engineering, wardrobe, hairdressing, make-up and prosthetics, post-production and specialist technical work.

Another way of conceptualising is to think of some roles as being directly about *making* film and other roles as *supporting* that creative act. The former are the direct hands-on film-making activities, whilst the latter ones includes activities such as distribution, marketing, showing and publicising film, everything from cinema management to budget administration. Both making and supporting are vital to the success of

Teamwork and concentration to get the shot exactly right

an industry that depends on generating revenue from a commercial (and artistic) endeavour.

Media careers can also be understood in terms of work contracting. A huge number of film people work as freelancers (to which we frequently refer in Part I). Recent research reveals that 63 per cent of film professionals had worked recently on a fixed-term contract, whilst 14 per cent had been employed as 'dailies' (given a daily rate for a job). Only 11 per cent had been permanent employees, and these were mainly in production.

Then there are the annual and daily work patterns in the film-making business. Unless you are a top professional, it is likely that you will experience a highly irregular working life. When working on a new production you may be expected to be on set for up to 12 hours a day, and occasionally longer if the shoot requires it. You may also find yourself working on commercials, training films, television broadcasts and other projects more often than big feature films. A recent survey showed that more than half of film-makers had actually worked fewer than 30 weeks on feature films in the previous year (Skillset, 2005).

Salaries also vary wildly, as you might expect with such a wide range of possible jobs in the industry. Sadly, but perhaps predictably, female-dominated areas such as hairdressing and costume report lower wages that the traditionally male-dominated technical roles. The big salaries (not including the obvious Mel Gibson/Cameron Diaz types) were reported to be in editing and post-production work.

It would be quite wrong to write about the film industry without acknowledging the very real threat of unemployment. More than one-third of film crew reported having been unemployed for more than 10 weeks in the previous year. Inevitably, the film business experiences peaks and troughs and you have to accept that it is not a stable, nine-to-five career.

Getting into the industry

You can be fairly sure that, no matter how talented you are, it is unlikely that you are going to see that perfect film job advertised in the local newspaper. You are going to have to think laterally and imaginatively about how you can break into the industry. Possibly you are a creative thinker anyway and that is why you are attracted to the work; if so, here is an opportunity to put that creativity to good use.

Almost half the entrants to the film industry in 2000 reported that they had done unpaid work before getting their first job. The message is clear: you must be prepared to do unpaid work to get a foot in the door. More than three-quarters of the surveyed professionals had worked in other audio-visual industries before they got into film, so you can expect to come into the industry almost through a side door rather than directly.

You should also be aware that the vast majority (81 per cent) of film workers had been recruited by word of mouth. That means that they were approached directly by a director or producer because they had been recognised as being an effective professional – and that is another very important message. You have read about the importance on network building in Part I, and here is a vivid portrayal of how important that really is.

So no one can pretend that it is going to be easy to break into film-making, but as our case studies show, it is possible and sometimes it is achieved through unlikely channels. You should think of creative, lateral approaches.

Many people get their first break into media work by becoming a 'runner' – a general dogsbody for a film-maker or crew. To be a runner you have to prove that you are absolutely reliable, incredibly adaptable and hard-working, can take unfair criticism and artistic tantrums in your stride, be unfailingly polite, pleasant, willing, highly organised, prepared to work 16-hour days in horrible conditions and generally be a complete angel. To be frank, this is not a role many graduates would deliberately choose for themselves, but you should consider it. Investing a year or so in being a runner gets you unmatched experience, a contact book crammed full of names and allows you to test whether this career really is for you. It would be a year well spent.

To get a job as a runner you should make sure you have a skills-based CV that makes explicit what you can offer the employer. You may have to take this in person to media companies and market yourself assertively to get a foot in the door. Addresses for companies to target can be found in media directories, which can be found in any good library.

The range and variety of supporting roles in film-making cannot be ignored. Almost every career you can imagine has its mirror on a film set. On major productions, for example, you will find medical teams, transport and logistics experts, musicians, accountants, personal trainers, animal handlers, chefs, personal assistants and linguists as well as the artists, writers, technical and creative personnel you would expect. If you can offer skills that are in short supply in one of these supporting jobs, you can get into the business by a side route.

Not everyone can walk into a job as a screenwriter, but being a smart and efficient touch typist and being able to do shorthand might get you in at a menial level in a film company. You probably wouldn't walk straight into casting, but administrative and people skills could get you into an assistant's job in which you can prove how indispensable you really are. A heavy goods vehicle (HGV) licence could get you on location quicker than sending hundreds of applications to work as a location manager.

Being a graduate, perhaps with relevant subject knowledge and a good range of employability skills, will be a bonus. But thinking laterally, being humble, hard-working, determined and willing could be what gives you that all-important first break into the industry.

Progression in film careers

The case studies will show you how unpredictable film work can be. You have to be lucky or able to create your own luck to succeed. There is absolutely no career path, no promotion ladder, no structured salary progression; it is a truly individualised industry. Having made that point, the sky really is the limit in that there are great opportunities to be had in the industry and all indications are that there will be even more opportunities in the future. The world seems to have a limitless appetite for visual entertainment, education and information, so it is a very promising sector for graduates with the right skills and attitudes.

Where to look for vacancies

The *Guardian* on Mondays is often cited as a useful source of vacancies, though these are mainly for experienced broadcasters, journalists and directors. *The Knowledge* (http://www.theknowledgeonline.com) is a directory of media, film and broadcasting contacts, but you will need to register to access it online. *Mandy* (http://www.mandy.com) has exciting UK and international vacancies for assistants and runners that will give you a real sense of the types of jobs available and the nature of the contracts. The best chance of finding work is contacts, word of mouth and referral. Use your lecturers, their contacts, graduates and other students as a starting point.

Case studies: Andrew Walkington

Andrew Walkington is a Film Director and Lecturer in Media Production at South Cheshire College in Crewe. He has had a complex and diverse career history which demonstrates how individuals have to be resilient and determined to make their dreams a reality in this industry.

How did you start film-making?

'From a young age, I knew I wanted to be involved somehow in film-making. When I was 18, I bought a second-hand VHS video camera and used it to make films with my friends. I discovered I had a flair for organising and realised that directing film was what I wanted to focus on.'

'After graduating with a degree in Theology and Drama, I was unemployed and I realised that if I was going to achieve my ambitions I would have to take matters very firmly into my own hands. I realised no one was going to 'discover' me and ask me to direct movies – however wonderful that would be. I approached the Manager of the Liverpool Playhouse and proposed putting on a production in their studio theatre. To my amazement, the Manager agreed. I created two productions with cast and crew working on a profit-share basis. Both productions did well, covering their costs and a little more. This experience was invaluable – I learnt that theatre is a business and must make a profit – and that people like to be paid!'

How did you build on this?

'I found myself unemployed again after a hideous experience working in a sausage factory and decided to apply for a vacancy in media sales. As

(Continued)

(Continued)

a trained actor and confident communicator I felt sure I could handle this work – it was basically selling advertising space in specialist professional journals. But I had no idea this would be the most constructive career-related experience I would ever have. I learnt crucial business-related skills that are so important in the creative industries; the ability to influence, negotiate and put your ideas over to the budget holders – those people who can make things happen. There are two ways to approach the film industry – as a professional or as an amateur. If you are happy to be an amateur and make films for fun, that's fine – but don't expect to make it into a career and don't assume you'll have an audience. If, however, you want to be a professional film-maker, then you have to realise that you will work to someone else's brief, the purpose is to maximise profit and you must have an audience.

'Armed with a year's experience in media sales, I had the business confidence to pitch my ideas to companies by focussing on how my projects would contribute to their profitability. This got me a job as a camera operator with a video-making company, where I quickly learnt the vital technical aspects of film-making. I learnt the hard way, yet again. The first job I was sent on I failed to record a full day of an event, costing the company thousands of pounds – really I should have been sacked on the spot. Needless to say, I'll never make that mistake again – always check you know how to operate equipment *before* you go on a shoot.'

What did you learn about the film industry?

'It is so different in the real, professional film production world, compared to being an amateur or what you read in the text books. Working for a high-pressure production company gave me a real understanding of the industry. I still had this idea that somehow my abilities would be recognised and that magically my career as a film director would take off. In fact, I found myself financially still insecure and unemployed again. There are no ladders to success in the business – you have to keep plugging at it long after it would seem sensible to give up. If you aren't tenacious and determined, you won't make it.'

How do you manage to teach and make films?

'In between teaching jobs I managed to pull together funding and a crew to shoot a short film starring David Baddiel, Brian Blessed and Phil Cool which was nominated for an award as best newcomer at the Liverpool Echo Arts Awards in 2000. I got a post as a Lecturer in Media Production at a top further education college in South Cheshire and once established, I implemented some of the skills honed in previous experience by initiating, obtaining funding for, and then creating a feature film involving students, professional actors and technical crew. This proved to be a fantastic opportunity for students to get hands-on experience of working with

(Continued)

Andrew hard at work with his students

professional actors in a real-life production, but the project was also highly valued by the actors concerned, who enjoyed the experience of interacting with the up-and-coming generation of film students. The film *Upstaged* gained international distribution and was shown at many festivals to critical acclaim.'

What advice would you offer aspiring film professionals?

'Don't think about the idea of breaking into film – that's not how it is. You don't get to work in film by answering adverts for jobs. You get in by managing your own career, making good contacts, being in the right place doing the right things. You cannot take opportunities, you have to *make* opportunities.'

What lessons can you offer from your own complicated career path?

'You have to realise that the film industry is a business, not a club for people to be creative in. You must possess key technical skills such as understanding the basic mechanics of a shoot and you must appreciate the business aspects. Tenacity, enthusiasm, complete determination and a

(Continued)

(Continued)

long-term view are absolutely essential. In a way, everyone involved in filming needs to have the skills of a producer; that is, to be able to look outwards from the creativity towards the market and the audience.'

What is it that helped you in achieving the success that you have?

'Wherever I am, whatever I am doing and whoever is paying, I think of myself as self-employed. I manage myself and my career. I want to help young people to avoid all those crazy mistakes I made during my career, to give them the advice, skills and support they need and that I never had. Many of my students are already working successfully in the industry and earning good money – that is a big motivator.'

Case study: Joe Withers

Joe Withers is a more recent graduate who left university in 2003 with a degree in Film and Media and a little practical experience of film-making. He wanted to work in film and discovered that going freelance was the answer to finding a range of flexible and interesting opportunities.

My degree included history and theory, not practical media, but whilst at university I found time to get involved in making a short film with a fellow student. I also volunteered for work experience on a film being made locally, which eventually led to me being offered some paid work as a locations assistant with a production company when I graduated.

Although the job was for only two and a half months, I quickly discovered that while such practical tasks as clearing people and unwanted cars from the streets are essential jobs during filming, I wanted to do something a bit more creative. I applied for more work experience and this time worked alongside the Art Director on the film *Chicken Tikka Masala*. Eventually I had enough confidence to apply for an ITV training scheme where I was asked to pitch ideas for a 5–10 minute film to a panel of interviewers.

Fortunately, my idea was accepted and a few more short-term film contracts later, I was approached by the director of a Lancashire-based film organisation, who wanted me to help set up a mobile film company. After several months touring rural areas and setting up screenings in the Lake District, I moved to London and worked on a small budget film there before returning North in search of more work. I applied for training with Media Training North West, an organisation which, amongst other things, helps freelancers to develop their skills. This was an excellent opportunity since, not only did they offer me quality training, I also received a wage.

Now three years after I left university, I am working on the BBC television drama *New Street Law*. I applied for the job, sent in a CV and following an

(Continued)

Joe Withers

interview, I secured a six-month paid contract as a production assistant. I feel that I have managed to create a niche for myself doing something which I am really enjoying.

It would be true to say that working in media production is not the most secure career in the world: the hours are long and pay is intermittent. You are always conscious of the fact that you might only work 40 weeks out of 52. On the positive side though, this is a very sociable job and I really enjoy working with the rest of the crew. All my meals are supplied and we do get invited to lots of parties!

Joe's advice

I would say to anyone who is about to begin their career – try to get some work experience at university. Be prepared to move. You should offer to work for free to start with and when you do manage to find work experience or paid work, take advantage of any spare time and ask if you can have some training.

Resources

www.ft2.org.uk/ – Ft2 is a training provider for freelance work in broadcasting and film:

Jobs and vacancies

www.theknowledgeonline.com/
www.grapevinejobs.co.uk
www.ideasfactory.com/

Careers advice and information

www.skillset.org/careers/
Guardian Media Directory (annual Guardian Newspapers Ltd.)

NINE Television

This chapter is written by Paul Egglestone, a senior lecturer and course leader of an International Documentary MA. He teaches television to undergraduates and postgraduate students as well as making television programmes and writing music. A former producer with experience of working for BBC, ITV and Sky on regional and national programming, he now focuses on international documentary and digital content generation for broadband and mobile dissemination.

The broadcasting industry

Browsing the average television schedule provides a reasonable introduction to the huge range and types of television programme production. A typical night of programming kicks off at 6.00 p.m. with BBC's national news programme followed by regional news. At 7.00 p.m. there is sitcom with *Open all Hours* followed by the BBC's flagship current affairs offering *Real Story*. At 9.00 p.m. there's a 'landmark' documentary with *Ocean Odyssey*, whilst over on BBC2 there's classy drama with *The Line of Beauty*. ITV has two hours of drama before its live hit show *X Factor*, whilst Channel 4 starts its evening with Matt Groening's animation *The Simpsons*.

And that's just the line-up on four UK terrestrial channels. As Sky TV announces its 8-millionth subscriber, 15 million homes now have satellite or cable TV. There are over 200 channels on Sky's digital platform. Combine them with NTL and Telewest's cable TV, add in existing terrestrial channels and UK audiences can access over 3,000 hours of television every day – from soap and sport to shopping. With such high audience penetration and almost 60 per cent of the population owning two or more television sets, it would seem these are the halcyon days of television. Over the last half century, television has become an 'industry' in the old – fashioned sense of the word – making products, marketing and distributing them nationally and internationally. As an industry, it offers a bewildering range of employment opportunities on either side of the camera, and the huge range of television-related jobs can make the initial decision to pursue a career in television seem a little daunting.

Concentration and technical ability is important in the media

If you are interested in getting a job in television, what follows will help you to focus your energy and resources appropriately. It concentrates on a job in television production rather than those in associated areas like production accountancy, programme sales or location catering, which all demand their own slightly different set of skills and qualifications.

As the television schedule provides an overview of the many different types of television programmes, it is a reasonable starting point for making a first television career choice. It may seem obvious that working in animation on a programme like *The Simpsons* will require a different set of skills than, say, shooting live action for a drama production – but it may be less obvious that there's an equally big gulf between factual programming (news and documentaries) and entertainment (shows like ITV's *X Factor* or C4's *Big Brother*) and even live

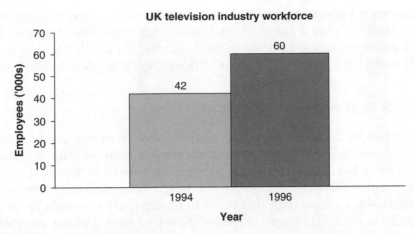

UK television industry workforce

programming for sport or studio-based magazine-style production. There is a difference between working in TV 'news', dealing with facts, constantly under pressure of tight deadlines, and working in drama, dealing with fiction, working with writers and actors and getting the period detail right. The decision about which 'genre' or type of television programming you would like to work in is an important one. Whilst your initial induction into any genre may be fairly general, as you immerse yourself in your chosen field and become a specialist, you also inevitably close off some options on route.

There are also very specific roles related to some genres. News programmes require news editors who would be a bit redundant in drama. Equally, a studio shoot will need an assistant floor manager, but the location-based documentary crew definitely won't.

Content or craft?

Whilst it's a bit of an artificial divide, you will need to decide whether you want to end up responsible for the ideas behind programmes (the content), or whether you'd prefer a role as part of a team that works in the background to get the production on air (the craft). For example, a news reporter or a television producer will come up with an original idea. They'll then commission a range of production services to help realise it. A big drama production will require a director, assistant director, director of photography, sound engineer, lighting director, camera operators, writers, composers, VT editors, make-up artists, animators and so on.

The excellent StartinTV.com (which you'll find on the web at www. startinTV.com/whichTVjobforme.php) lists a range of jobs in television spanning all genres and every level of production. There are also brief case studies from a range of television personnel who describe their jobs and how they got started in the business. It's worth a look if you're still undecided about which area of television you'd like to work in.

Roles and skills in television

Once you've decided which part of television work you might want to go for, you need to work out the best way to achieve your ambitions. Television has a long tradition of starting people at the bottom and encouraging them to learn on the job. In television journalism there still seems to be a career path that starts in newspapers and ends up in television via radio. However, there are plenty of stories about production secretaries becoming series producers after proving their worth on previous productions. Equally, there are senior editors in Soho's facilities houses who started off as 'runners', making coffee and backing up programmes to hard disks overnight.

Appropriate courses which are accredited and recognised by the industry are usually very focussed. Despite this, there is no absolute guarantee of getting a job having completed the course. It is an extremely competitive business, and only the most committed and determined succeed. It's about having passion for television and the self-belief that you have something to bring to the party. And when it comes to the job interview – or BBC 'board' – it is as much about you as a person and how you demonstrate your passion and commitment.

Focussing on a very particular role within television may appear a little limiting given the broad range of jobs available. Whatever television job you decide to pursue, the advice is the same – concentrate 100 per cent of your energy and resources on where they'll be most effective in helping you achieve your ambition.

Here are two case studies of recent graduates, one from a BA undergraduate course and one from an MA postgraduate course.

Case study: Mar Cabra

Mar Cabra graduated from Uclan in 2004 after successfully completing her Journalism BA (Hons). She currently works as a trainee journalist for CNN in Spain. Television is synonymous with technology, and Mar Cabra's current job requires her detailed knowledge of IT to complement her editorial skills and writing ability. She produces news packages, called 'oovs' ('out of vision' stories – video news clips with a script for a studio presenter to read over the pictures).

(Continued)

How did you break into a top company like CNN?

'Whilst I was doing my degree in Preston I did some work experience for Liverpool FC TV as a camera operator, floor manager and auto cue controller. It might not seem related to journalism, but I learnt a lot about sports journalism from watching. Before going to CNN I did some work experience at the BBC in the UK and got a two-month contract afterwards. I'm certain that having "BBC" on my CV has opened a lot of doors. I'm not saying it's only the name that counts, but it helps'

Describe what you do.

'Once I arrive in the office the first thing I do is open Avid's 'iNews' system and check the running order. This is the most important part of the day when I'll find out what stories I might be doing, and what my colleagues are doing – then we're not duplicating each other's efforts. From then on, I can propose stories we could do. I try to find the stories of the day, not only through agencies (Reuters and AP are the best for international news), but also through three different websites: BBC.co.uk (they are a bit slow refreshing the information, but always right on numbers!), cnn.com (good info too, I work for them!) and elpais.es (the most read Spanish newspaper, good quality). I'll also source stories from APTN (Associated Press Television News), Sky News and CNN's other outputs.

'The news editor will set the news agenda for the day and tell me which stories I must cover. Once I've viewed the video images I'll edit them using Avid News-Cutter before writing the accompanying script.'

What training did you receive?

'The production process is similar to the one I trained in at university. First I prepare the story, then I'll find contributors before going to the location and shooting the piece. When I'm producing a location story it's very useful to have a clear sense of the images I need to tell the story. I try to write the script as soon as I finish filming, wherever I am: in the taxi, in the car coming back to the studios. It's hard work. On my six-hour shift I'm likely to produce a news package and four oovs easily. It's busy – that's what I like about it.'

What do you like about your job?

'I shoot, write, edit and record voice-over for every package I make. I have learnt web design programmes (like Dreamweaver or Flash), as different media merge. It sounds tough, but I see the future this way. We will have to update our knowledge constantly. It may be difficult, but it sounds quite fun too, doesn't it?'

What advice would you give to aspiring TV journalists?

'I think the best advice is never to stop working. You might not get what you want straight away, or you might not work exactly where you'd like, but you will always learn something.

Case study: Kris Jepson

Kris Jepson is a contract producer for Sky News in London. He graduated from the Dept of Journalism at the University of Central Lancashire in 2004 with an MA in Broadcast Journalism. As a contract producer he is responsible for delivering news generated by the Sky News production teams to a variety of outputs nationally and internationally.

How did you land your first job?

'After completing my degree I applied for the MA broadcast course at the University of Central Lancashire. It has a very good reputation and offers a 'conversion' course for anyone with a degree in pretty much any discipline to train as a journalist. As well as learning the core skills of journalism like spotting a story and writing it up appropriately for radio and television, you learn about public administration and you get a recognised law qualification. I also made a documentary for my MA project. It was on the Chinese cocklers who died doing their job out on Morecambe Bay. As well as being an interesting subject, the film got me a couple of jobs as an assistant producer on news items for BBC and Channel 4 news and an interview at Sky News, where I've been working since.'

What skills do you need for the work?

'You need to be a good communicator and to be able to think on your feet. You need to know your media law. You have to be accurate and precise in your reporting. Keep up to date with reporting restrictions and the legalities of reporting and investigating. You'll need good writing skills. Script writing for TV news, particularly network news, has to be concise. Simplicity is the key. You'll need a good grasp of current affairs, an awareness of politics and political modes, methods and structures. Increasingly, you need to be familiar with new technologies and their effect on journalism.'

What advice would you offer to someone wanting to be a journalist?

'There's little point in taking a course that only prepares you for the current needs of the industry. The smart money will always look one step ahead to try to spot future trends. News is a multimedia industry now. You can see your pictures and reports anywhere in the world. Soon you will be able to access the news everywhere – on the tube, in e-newspapers you can fold up in your pocket, in service stations and on planes. Sky News has an enviable reputation for leading in news innovation, but its journalists need to keep abreast of the latest technology and the ways they can improve if Sky is to maintain its cutting edge.'

Was it competitive to get in?

'I found the business very competitive. Most of my journalist colleagues have got degrees and many of them have done a postgraduate course as

(Continued)

well. Whilst there's no set way to get into it, a qualification from a recognised course helps. There are ads for journalism jobs in the *Guardian* on Mondays – and good courses offer a placement in TV news where students get to see how it works.'

What specifically helped you to get in?

'I applied for a well-regarded Master's course (at Uclan) and I picked an interesting subject for my final MA film. My experience gained doing the documentary project on my course gave me a really good 'calling card' to see commissioning editors and potential employers. Whilst making my MA film, I worked with news teams at the BBC and C4 producing items on the cockle pickers' deaths for both channels. Then I started networking. I managed to get an appointment to see Kevin Sutcliffe, who was the commissioning editor at C4 *Dispatches*, as well as meeting Nick Broomfield, the documentary film-maker, at the Sheffield International Documentary Festival to discuss his cockle pickers' film (awarded a BAFTA in 2007). The job at Sky came up and I took my film and a show reel to the interview. They offered me work and I've been here ever since.'

A foot in the door

Getting a 'foot in the door' is the first and most difficult step on the road to working in television. That's why courses offering structured placements are good. As well as giving you the chance to experience programme production from the inside and make your own assessment of the job you'd most like to do, they provide the opportunity to meet and talk to people in the industry. If you haven't had this opportunity built into a course, make sure you get experience by referring to Chapter 5 Work Experience.

Many jobs in television are never advertised to the wider world. Chance conversations and informal professional networks often prove the best grapevine for who is hiring and what projects are coming up. If you are lucky enough to get experience at the BBC for example, you can access the in-house paper *Ariel* which always has a couple of pages of jobs that you'd be unlikely to see anywhere outside the corporation. *Broadcast*, the weekly newspaper for the television business, has a jobs section, but the best way to use *Broadcast* is to look at the news sections and find out which companies have just won commissions for more programming. They may be hiring staff. It may be worth buying the *Guardian* newspaper on Monday, too. The *Guardian* has a bit of a stranglehold on the media jobs advertising market. There's no other national newspaper with more media jobs pages and few other publications outside specialist magazines and in-house newsletters that bring together as many employers looking for new recruits. The *Guardian* also runs an annual media careers fair that's pretty well attended by the industry and worth a look – even if it's only to 'suss out' the opposition.

The broadcasting industry is competitive to enter because many people like the idea of working in the media. Some see it as a quick way to amass a fortune – but alas, precisely because so many people would like to work in television, salaries are not fantastic, though they are generally better than in newspapers. A graduate can expect to start on £15–£20K. The top jobs have six-figure salaries attached to them, with people like Jeremy Paxman earning well over a million pounds a year.

Salaries are directly related to where in the organisation you work. Television is a difficult business to get into, and it's also difficult to get on once you're in. But there are structures or 'career ladders' you can climb once you're in. If you start as a researcher you can progress to assistant producer, then to producer. If you're a reporter you may eventually want to become a senior broadcast journalist before becoming a correspondent or a news editor. Some journalists do a stint as reporters or editors then move into management or department heads. Others may become executive producers or even channel controllers. At the higher level there are obviously fewer opportunities and it is extremely competitive, so some people set up their own independent production companies, making programmes they can sell back to their former company bosses. You are just as likely to secure a job with an 'indy' (an independent production company) as you are with one of the major broadcasters.

Like Kris and Mar, those who succeed have generally chosen the appropriate degree or post-grad. course, done a series of work placements and produced a show-reel example of their work. They've probably worked in a related field during their holidays and they would have prepared for their job interview by watching the programme they'd like to work on and offered a few ideas about how to improve the output at interview. Before embarking on their job search they made sure they had the right qualifications, skills and abilities to do the job applied for. This in itself can be a fairly complex task as there's very little standardisation of roles across the industry, and yet employers expect that you'll have the right skills for them.

A television reporter will have a different set of skills to the news editor, who'll have different skills to the cameraman – or the person on the input desk. There'll be some crossover of some roles when it comes to story selection and story-telling. Most television news editors have been reporters, so they understand the way it works.

It is difficult to move straight into television journalism without a relevant degree or, more likely, a postgraduate degree. There are traineeships occasionally, but these are hotly contested and consequently may be a bit of a lottery. You could try working as a 'runner' (general dog's body) for a television company if you're really unsure about whether you want to end up in television but runners tend to end up in the craft-based jobs rather than those dealing with editorial.

What skills must a TV reporter have?

A television reporter needs a nose for a good story and the confidence to ask hard questions that people might not want to answer. They need to be able to win people over and persuade them to appear on television – and sometimes say things that might upset a few people. Television is about sound and vision, so they need to know how to tell the story visually. They need to be able to write because a story will need a script and a cue (the piece that the presenter reads from the studio to introduce each item). They need to be able to make difficult decisions quickly. They must know their media law very well and understand how government works.

Increasingly, television reporters are editing their own video material too. This used to be done by dedicated 'craft' editors.

Case study: Clive Jones

Clive Jones is Managing Director of the Independent News Group (ING), which supplies ITN news for ITV and C4.

'Desktop editing will be the norm at ITV within three years. Video journalists will be the core of the newsroom and a new grade of 'creative technicians' will perform the traditional 'craft' roles'. The future of ING news is undoubtedly interactive. The red button click will offer breadth and depth beyond the current constraints of a time-based news report.

'Personal Video Recorders (PVRs) will also enable people to select the news – even the items they want. And, of course, there are plans to offer news content for mobile phones.'

Television journalism is changing. If you want to make a career in television you should equip yourself with a range of the new skills employers will expect all their latest recruits to have. Core skills required to work in the medium do not change, and a good journalist must get excited about telling stories. But there are some practical ways anyone wishing to work in the field can make themselves more employable for the future:

- You must be able to edit.
- You must develop camera skills. There is a trend towards video journalism pushed by the BBC and ITV companies alike in the UK.
- If you want to work for a bureau abroad you will need to speak more than one language.

Just as Clive Jones identified the changing nature of ING, Mark Thompson, Director General of the BBC, is making similar noises about spending a large proportion of the licence fee on his plan to prepare the BBC for what he sees as the new digital era. This was the theme of his speech at the Edinburgh Television Festival in 2005: '"On demand" is the core of the digital debate and may even change what we mean by "broadcasting". The BBC must be at the forefront of developments." He continued, 'I believe that a broadly based, multi-media BBC with a brand that everyone knows, along with great, relevant content that everyone can use and which demonstrably creates public value, will actually make more sense than it does today.'

Sky TV is also coming to terms with the digital era and already offers an interactive news service. There are plans to develop further their news content for mobile phones, PDAs, broadband and so on. As technology develops, critics suggest there will be fewer jobs in television. It is more likely that television jobs will migrate to, and converge with, jobs in related fields like online and broadband content creation.

Television is a dynamic industry. Consequently, anyone wishing to work in television must be prepared to adapt to new challenges whilst recognising that the essence of journalism doesn't really change. The way it is done is changing all the time. Television journalists are expected to be multi-skilled.

Television companies

If you want to work in television, the obvious places to head for are the BBC, CNN, Sky and ITV's Independent News Group. Then there are news agencies like Reuters, Associated Press Television News (APTN) and the European News Exchange (ENEX). Within each of these organisations there are divisions or departments with specialists covering politics, health and sport. There are also independent production companies making news and documentaries for a range of television channels – they all need journalists too.

In the UK, there are TV journalists in local news stations like Granada covering the northwest of England, or BBC North covering Newcastle, Tyneside and into Cumbria. ITV has about 16 regional news stations and the BBC have divided the country up slightly differently but match the ITV coverage. Most network news stations are London based – Sky News is at Osterley in West London. News correspondents could be pretty much anywhere in the world. Sky is a big operation but the BBC has bureau staffed with journalists all over the world.

Relevant courses

Most news editors will expect you to have a degree or post-grad. diploma/MA from a BJTC (Broadcast Journalism Training Council) accredited course. There are a number of these across the UK and there's more information about the range of courses and where they're located on the BJTC website (www.bjtc.org.uk/).

A post-grad. conversion course provides an opportunity for graduates from almost any discipline to acquire the necessary skills to work in journalism. BJTC accreditation ensures that courses offer relevant industry skills, law and public administration and insist on work placements as part of the course. There's little merit pursuing courses that are not BJTC accredited if you know you want to be a journalist.

There are a range of short courses offered by credible training and broadcasters like the BBC and the British Film Institute. These courses will typically be intensive and extremely focussed. If you feel you're likely to prefer this route, make sure your training organisation offers a recognised qualification at the end of the course.

The buzz!

There are plenty of jobs that are easier – certainly many that are better paid. And there are jobs that don't expect you to sacrifice your weekends and evenings. But how many jobs afford the opportunity to travel the world, meet interesting people and make films about them? The programmes I've made have taken me to Africa, India and America, as well as throughout Europe many times. I've flown in helicopters, travelled in speedboats, hitched rides with militia, slept in the jungle, always get an AAA pass at festivals and had the chance to work with some of the most talented creative and fun people around. Why would anyone *not* want a job in television?

Resources

www.bbctraining.com/television.asp

www.bfi.org.uk/education/

www.city.ac.uk/ell/

www.skillset.org/ – Skillset Careers is the specialist careers information, advice and guidance (IAG) service for broadcast, film, video, interactive media and photo imaging. They are industry and publicly funded and work with trade unions, trade associations and industry employers to improve the quality of information and advice given in schools, further and higher education, and through public agencies. Skillset also provides careers advice direct to individuals.

www.productionbase.co.uk/ – More than 1,000 film and television jobs go through Productionbase every month.

www.broadcastfreelancer.com/ – Sister to the TV industry magazine 'Broadcast', this site offers job advertisements and industry information.

www.bbc.co.uk/jobs/ – Biggest of the UK broadcasters and a major employer. The site also offers careers advice and lists details of careers events and so on.

www.startinTV.com/ – Careers advice and a CV-hosting service. Also job advertisement.

www.ukscreen.com/ – The film and music network.

shootingpeople.org/ – The US and UK indie film community. Predominantly a networking area with regular email bulletins on jobs.

TEN Radio

This chapter is written by Andrew Edwards, senior lecturer in Radio, Trinity and All Saints College, Leeds. Andrew joined the BBC in 1989 and has since worked as a reporter, producer, senior producer and assistant editor. He has presented the breakfast show at BBC Radio Leeds since 1995.

Setting the scene

Radio is a powerful, uniquely personal medium. It has an intimacy, an ability to speak directly to *you*, one to one. You can listen to the radio and do something else at the same time: work, cook, drive, watch a football match, try to sleep. Recent technological advances mean that radio is becoming far more flexible. You can listen to a live cricket commentary through a computer anywhere in the world; you can download an MP3 version of a programme onto a portable listening device little bigger than a human finger; you can listen to the radio through your television set. Digital broadcasting (DAB, Digital Audio Broadcasting) is with us, although – unlike television – there are no immediate plans to switch off the old analogue network. The number of stations is multiplying. You no longer need a transmitter and expensive studios, but can broadcast via the Internet from a back bedroom kitted out with relatively cheap equipment. You can podcast to a niche audience of 12 or, potentially, 12 million. In radio one person can take an idea all the way from first concept to broadcast: recording an interview, editing and mixing it, handing it over for transmission. For the right person, it is a hugely exciting career. But how you get in, and, once you are in, how do you get on?

Be under no illusions: it is competitive. To succeed you will need to love radio. Listen to as much as you can: the more variety, the better. Try speech radio if you usually listen to music, football commentaries if you have never been to a match in your life. But you will also need to be really determined to make this your career. In employment terms, radio is not a big business. About 20,000 people work in the UK radio industry: 43 per cent are women, 7.4 per cent are from ethnic minorities, 1 per cent are disabled, 19 per cent are freelance (Skillset, 2004).

A typical studio at a radio station

If you think this is a quick route to showbiz megabucks, think again. A news and sports reporter for a successful commercial radio station might earn £12,500 a year, having completed three years at university and perhaps a year's postgraduate training. The starting salary for a trainee manager working for a fast food chain is likely to be twice that.

There are thousands of students on media-related courses in the UK – more studying the subject, at any one time, than there are jobs in the whole of the radio industry. It is a telling statistic which should make you take stock. Doing a media studies course will not, in itself, get you a radio job. The more specific and focussed your education (for example, industry accredited journalism training or electrical engineering), the more likely it is to lead directly to work. However, many people with seemingly relevant degrees will not get work in radio, while many who have studied something completely different but done radio with a passion in their spare time will succeed. It is what you are like as a person, how committed you are and – there is no shying away from it – how good you are (or have the potential to be) which will mark you out. Being a radio star in the making does not necessarily go along with getting good marks in the classroom. We have all heard stories of people with golden voices but little training who get work ahead of someone with excellent qualifications, but a nervous manner and a weak on-air voice.

One of the most common questions, particularly at careers events, is 'What qualifications do I need?'. It is the obvious thing to ask, but is also remarkably difficult to answer. If you want to become a teacher or a dentist there is a defined education and career path. I have worked in the main production office of a busy radio station with two experienced producers on either side of me: one left school at 16 with virtually no qualifications, the other has a Cambridge University doctorate. They have very different skills and qualities, personal and professional, but both were essentially doing the same job. What they share is a love of radio and the ideas and creativity to make it happen. It is common to find a DJ with a huge knowledge of music and the gift of the gab but few academic qualifications working alongside a journalist who has just finished a postgraduate diploma course in broadcast journalism at university.

Roles in radio

Broadly speaking, mainstream radio divides into two: the BBC, the public service broadcaster funded by the licence fee, and commercial radio, which makes money by selling advertising. In 2006 there were five BBC analogue national networks, BBC stations for Scotland, Wales and Northern Ireland, 40 BBC local radio stations, 281 analogue commercial stations (local and regional), three national commercial stations and an ever-expanding number of digital and online stations. All the national stations are based in London, although this could change with the possible move of the news and sports channel BBC Radio Five Live to Manchester. An increasing number of BBC network programmes are already produced outside the capital. Local and regional stations are spread across the country. As you would expect, the biggest centres of population have the most competitive radio markets with more stations and more jobs.

Presentation

This is the first role everyone thinks of, but a radio station is about far more than its presenters/DJs. You are also highly unlikely, unless you are very talented or very lucky, to walk straight into an on-air job. Most people start at the bottom and work up. Get as much experience as you can on college or university stations or on hospital radio. Presenters are the front line troops, the voices you hear on the air. These also tend to be the roles which everyone fancies before they think about what the job actually entails. Breakfast shows might be fun and might get the biggest audiences, but would you really want to get up at four in the morning? It sounds obvious, but music stations demand people who have a passion for what they play, whether that is rock music on the Kerrang commercial stations or Bach and Beethoven on BBC Radio 3. Equally, a hard news programme will normally be hosted by a well-informed journalist. However, there are countless examples of people moving across the radio dial. Simon Bates, once a lynchpin of BBC Radio 1 at the young end of the market, now broadcasts to the older end on the national commercial station Classic FM. Nowadays most presenters operate their own equipment. There are not lots of jobs for technical operators who do not ever speak on air. A radio desk might look like the flight deck of a jet, but if you can learn to drive a car, you can learn to drive a radio programme!

Production

The ideas people. They decide what goes into programmes and how best to convert those ideas into riveting radio. They also nurture and cajole the on-air talent – the presenters. Getting the right material and the appropriate sound for a station needs creativity and a real understanding of the audience. Many commercial stations do not have separate programme producers, except perhaps for breakfast, but a speech-based BBC local station will have a range of broadcast assistants and producers – journalists and non-journalists – who are involved with setting up and putting out programmes.

Journalism

Every radio station in the UK broadcasts news bulletins. They are the one area of output they all have in common. A small commercial station might have just two journalists: one reading the morning bulletins, the other looking after the afternoon and early evenings. A talk-based BBC station, such as Five Live, has scores of news and sports journalists working round the clock. Journalists need to be snappy, quick writers. They usually also have good on-air voices. They need to understand the law and the way the world works (which council is responsible for emptying the bins or running the schools?). Many will have studied on courses accredited by the Broadcast Journalism Training Council (www.bjtc.org.uk), which includes industry and educational representatives.

Technical and IT

Not perhaps the most glamorous side of the business, but these are the vitally important people who keep the station on air, providing broadcast engineering services and information technology support. As broadcasting becomes more and more IT based, this really requires degree-level training or a long apprenticeship.

Administration

Like any other business, radio needs backroom staff on the switch-board, making sure everyone gets paid and dealing with the smooth running of the office. As one radio boss puts it, 'It's still admin, but it's much more fun with us than it is in the planning department of the local council!'

Management

Again, hardly likely to be the first job you walk into. These people lead the station, with responsibility for its overall sound and strategy, its future direction, its staff, its successes and its problems. Who *can* do the drivetime show when the presenter rings in sick at 90-minutes' notice? Ideally, they have superb people and communications skills. They will give feedback to the on- and off-air teams and will recruit staff. In commercial radio, managers are normally called programme controllers or directors (PCs or PDs); in the BBC, managing editors and assistant editors.

There are also a number of roles specific to commercial radio.

Airtime sales staff understand advertising and radio. They are able to communicate effectively with would-be clients from all levels of business. People working in sponsorship and promotions require similar skills to sales, but also have an ability to come up with and sell (both internally and externally) great ideas.

There are two distinct roles in **commercial production**: the writer and the producer. 'Writer' is something of a misnomer, as actually writing copy is only about one-quarter of the job. You need an under-standing of advertising and an ability to write for the ear (as opposed to the eye). You also need to be able to talk to a prospective client and help them identify their advertising needs. You have to sell your scripts and then cast and direct the ads. The producers of advertisements are also directors of talent and sensitive writers: skilled with people and digital editing.

Getting into radio

Getting your foot in the door is often the most difficult step. Once you are in, you can talk to people, read the internal newsletter and hear about those jobs which never get advertised to the wider world. Or, as is more often the case, you make the tea. Then, when someone is on holiday or ill, you get asked to do the job for real: taking the calls on a busy phone-in or helping the DJ on a public appearance in a shopping centre. So what gets you that first interview or weekend of work experience? If you are on a course with a vocational element (for example, media) or one which concentrates on a specific medium (such as radio) or set of skills (for example, journalism), you will probably be going on at least one industry placement. This is a chance to find out what really happens and, if you are lucky, to impress them with your work. But what qualities are required? How important is formal training? If you are lucky enough to get an interview, what really gets you noticed? Here two successful radio professionals give you their thoughts.

Case study: Martyn Healy

Martyn Healy is the Brand Managing Director of Galaxy, a group of stations playing dance and rhythm and blues music in the Northeast, Yorkshire, Manchester and Birmingham. He joined Pennine Radio in Bradford in 1982 as 'early morning dogsbody, writing gags for the breakfast show host and compiling traffic reports' after graduating from Trinity and All Saints University College in Leeds.

What do you need to get into radio?

'You need a love of the medium bordering on the anorakic. You need to be almost obsessive about it. Radio is full of people who started at the bottom. But you've got to really want it. Demonstrate that by volunteering wherever possible. Following my degree I was willing to work unsocial hours and work way beyond my paid-for hours by being helpful and not getting in the way. I am more likely to take a punt on a non-formally trained individual if they have the passion and personal skills. And for technical jobs with lots of applicants, I find most people are trained to a similar standard. Once again it comes down to the extras that you can bring to a team in the form of interpersonal skills, passion and drive. One piece of excellent advice you often hear is to combine your formal training with a life outside the classroom: I've found that many applicants have combined their degrees with a high level of hands-on experience. These are the people best suited to securing a full time gig.'

So, when you are finally sitting in front of Martyn Healy, trying to convince him that this is the job for you, how *do* you clinch it?

'Be outstanding, well prepared and think of your interview as an open opportunity. The fact you are there says the station thinks you could handle the gig. It also says that the other five or six candidates could too. It's your mission to be outstanding at the interview. Literally stand out from the rest (in a positive way!). That means doing the little, obvious things well. Be on time, be clean and presentable and be prepared. If necessary, listen to the station 24/7 and drop in an intelligent comment about something you have heard. Know what you want. Write it down in precise terms. Then go for it!'

(Continued)

Martyn Healy

Case study: Phil Roberts

Phil Roberts is the Managing Editor of BBC Radio Leeds. He is a prime example of someone who has wanted to be involved with radio from an early age. He started in hospital radio at 13, presented the breakfast show on his hometown radio station in Wrexham for five years, where he was also station programme director, and then moved to a series of senior management positions in commercial radio.

How do you break into radio?

'Never be afraid to put your hand up to help with anything. My break came after making tea in a newsroom for six months before being asked to present a show. Be useful and believe in what you do passionately. Get curious about what matters to your audience in terms of talking points and stories. Ask yourself what would people be talking about in the pub that evening – what's important on the street and in your audience's homes.'

Although Phil did not study radio at college or university he has strong views about the value of courses:

(Continued)

(Continued)

'Formal training is essential to be a journalist, however, we are encouraging more varied educational routes to get into the BBC. Never let a lack of formal training put you off. Get some good work experience and always seek advice. The standard of people applying to us from media, radio and journalism degrees is generally good. However, the number of people who turn up for an interview with no knowledge of the radio station's output is staggering. Listen to the radio station via the web and have a view on the stories, the presenters and the content. Do your homework and really care about the output. That way you will get the job over the others.'

Like Martyn Healy, Phil Roberts believes that, with enough determination, *you* can break into this hugely competitive industry. Here are his top tips:

'Get experience and work hard. Skills can be learnt, but your attitude is not negotiable. It is that which will get you in the front door. If you're applying to a radio station, research who is in charge of the programmes or news and write to them personally. Never be afraid to ring them. People rarely do, and a good boss will take your call.'

Finally, if you get called to interview, what will get you that coveted job?

'Know the output; have an opinion; understand the local area; do your research. Keep on trying, never give up and really care about the output. But above all, be yourself and live a life outside of radio.'

Everyone you speak to will have a different story, full of pitfalls and pleasures. And at the start it can be really tough. That job in sales might seem very tempting after your fiftieth rejection letter. You may have to convince sceptical family and friends that it is a worthwhile, 'real' job. You may face the resistance of well-meaning but often ill-informed careers advisers. And, if you are honest, you may find that the hardest person to convince is yourself: Can I really do this? Do I want it enough?

Case study: Nicola Rees

Nicola Rees studied on the BA (Hons) Journalism course at the University of Central Lancashire in Preston. In her final year she specialised in radio journalism, leaving – in 2003 – with a degree accredited by the BJTC (Broadcast Journalism Training Council). She now has a staff job as a broadcast journalist at BBC Radio Leeds, the BBC local station serving West Yorkshire, and is a freelance presenter for the Yorkshire edition of the BBC1 television programme Inside Out.

(Continued)

What do you do?

'I report on various local news stories, events and activities, including live broadcasts on location, pre-recorded interviews and feature pieces. My role involves responding to breaking stories in West Yorkshire, and planning or self-generating future story ideas and prospects. I also do some bulletin reading and programme production.'

So, how important was your degree?

'It was very useful. It gave me a basic understanding of the various news mediums – TV, radio, online and print. There was a strong emphasis on the practical skills of reporting the news. We were encouraged to be hands-on as much as possible in our chosen medium, whether that was producing a website, filming your own news report or producing a radio programme. The radio studios, technical equipment and editing software were all excellent. Staff are extremely knowledgeable because all had previously worked in the industry. The weekly 'news days', where students took on the responsibility of reporters, presenters and producers, were invaluable.

'Formal training is important, but not essential. Work experience can be much more beneficial than lectures and seminars. I've met many excellent journalists and producers who started without formal training. Many of the skills and much of the experience don't come until you start your first job. There's only so much you can learn in the classroom. Having said that, there's so much competition for jobs these days that a degree is often a basic requirement for getting you an interview.'

What did you do to enhance your CV?

'I had a life outside the lecture theatre. As well as working in various jobs to pay my way through university, I built up a wide range of relevant experience from hospital radio to writing features in the match programmes for Preston North End football club. I started live news reading, first at a small restricted service licence (RSL) radio station and then, while still studying, as a weekend bulletin reader at a commercial radio station. I also worked for a local MP as a press and media liaison officer, gaining invaluable personal skills and learning about Westminster and office politics. It was often difficult to balance the conflicting demands of college work, paid for employment and relevant work experience. But this portfolio of experiences helped land me that all-important job interview.'

How did you get your first break?

'Having finished my degree, I applied like mad for anything and everything – sending my CV to almost every radio station in the country! I also pestered the contacts I'd made during my placement at BBC Radio Leeds, and after

(Continued)

(Continued)

Nicola Rees

a couple of months it paid off. I got an interview for a broadcast journalist's job in Leeds, and the rest is history.'

What advice would you give current students?

'Don't just sit back and expect the job to come to you – it will not. And use the contacts you have made. If guest speakers come in to speak to you, or if you go on a placement as part of your course, keep in touch with the people you have met. If you impress them – even if you are simply polite, personable and reliable – it might be you who gets that all-important call when someone is needed to cover a weekend shift at short notice!'

What makes you successful as a presenter?

'Be real, be yourself; being authentic on air is vitally important. You also need good interpersonal and communication skills to get the best from interviewees.'

Nicola's advice for anyone wanting to get a job in radio is simple:

- Get experience – as much of it as possible. Hospitals are always looking for volunteer radio presenters, and most commercial stations will not turn you down if you are offering your services for free.
- Be prepared to work hard and give up your weekends.

(Continued)

- If you get a placement or work experience, be enthusiastic and likeable!
- Find an experienced reporter to shadow.
- Try to come up with ideas for stories, and make sure you go out to do the piece yourself.
- Get your reports on the radio – it is great for a demo disc.
- Most of all, make contacts and keep in touch with them.

Case study: Mark Poyser

Mark Poyser also studied radio journalism at University. He is a broadcast journalist at Viking FM, the commercial radio station in Hull.

What do you do?

'I write, produce and read breakfast bulletins for two radio stations; Viking and its sister station Magic 1161AM. This is, in itself, a useful skill and typical of the flexibility you need. I often write for two different audiences, listening to two different radio stations, broadcasting from the same building, at the same time. I also face, every day, the early morning alarm call at 4.30 a.m. This may, just about, be showbiz, but it is certainly not glamorous on a frosty morning when you cannot get your old banger started and are due on air in half an hour!'

What skills do you need to be successful in radio?

'Good organisation, efficiency, quick thinking, decisiveness and a real sense for what makes good radio. If you're a journalist, you need a good knowledge of media law, current affairs and local issues. And it's vital to have the ability to 'see the story' and make fast decisions, to describe the world around you and paint pictures for the listener. In a world which lives by the clock, you have to be ready to work to deadlines. The 8 o'clock news is, by definition, at 8 o'clock. If you are ready with a perfectly crafted piece of work at three minutes past, you are late, and the bulletin will probably be over.'

What helped you get in?

'My journalism degree was extremely useful. Specialising in radio in my third year really prepared me for the field I wanted to go into. Going on a placement gave me valuable experience and the impression I left at Radio Aire enabled me to get my job at Viking, which is owned by the same radio group.

'As a student I had fun producing and playing around with audio, and the skills I learnt then are still as valuable now. You need to know what you're doing, so it is very important. But I think you learn better and quicker by

(Continued)

(Continued)

Mark Poyser

actually doing it. That's why the structure of my degree course – with lots of practical work – was so useful. That training continues now with, for example, regular voice training sessions and legal refreshers. It keeps you on your toes – after all, no one's perfect!'

If you are lucky, you might find that your job allows you to indulge your passion. Mark loves sport:

'I've known since I was about 14 that I wanted to work in radio. I've always wanted to be a football commentator. Now I also have a lot of responsibilities when it comes to Viking's sports output. I interview players and managers from our four main football teams (Hull City, Doncaster Rovers, Scunthorpe United and Grimsby Town), as well as the two big rugby league teams in the area, Hull FC and Hull KR. I also cover matches. I've been to the Millennium Stadium in Cardiff for the Challenge Cup Final when Hull FC beat the Leeds Rhinos.'

(Continued)

Mark has already tasted the rewards that can come from making excellent radio. In 2005 his news team won a prestigious Sony Gold Award for a special feature on binge drinking:

'Viking's never won a Gold before and it was so unexpected. The ceremony was the best night of my life. But working life does not always go to plan. You need to be prepared to do jobs such as going out to do vox pops, a series of short interviews with members of the public on the issue of the day. It could be anything from whether you should be allowed to smoke in public places to whether you prefer chicken korma or fish and chips as your Friday night takeaway. It's amazing how rude and unhelpful people can be. And once I drove all the way from Hull to Teeside Crown Court for a major hearing for a case in our patch – only to find out, when I got there, that it was at Sheffield Crown Court! I was not the most pleasant of people to work with that afternoon when I got back three hours later.'

Here are Mark Poyser's top tips:

- Be yourself. In an interview do not pretend to be someone you are not. If you wrongly claim to be an expert about something, you will get found out.
- Be ready to learn and listen to people more experienced than you. They have so much to teach you.
- Be willing to do anything at the start. If you refuse to do something, someone else will take it on.
- Be keen and be flexible. You have got to take your chance whenever and wherever it comes along.

Have you got what it takes?

Radio is not the right career for you if you vaguely fancy a career in the media. It is a hugely competitive business. But if you love *listening* to the radio – all sorts of stations, at all times of day – and are excited at the thought of *making* radio, this might well be the career for you. Be honest with yourself. You will probably have to put in lots of work, for little or no pay, to get that necessary first break. Your enthusiasm, your passion for radio and your desire to succeed in your chosen field are often more important than what you study.

If you want to be a journalist, consider an industry accredited undergraduate or postgraduate course. There are also excellent practical courses in further education colleges, but do not be fooled into thinking that just because one is offered (for example in practical, technical radio skills) there is necessarily a shortage of skills in that area. Some courses exist because there is a demand from students to study them, rather than a requirement from the industry for training. Above all, get as much hands-on experience as you can.

Have you started looking to see what jobs are on offer? The first thing that will probably strike you is how few advertisements there are for radio work. The *Guardian* newspaper has the biggest selection of advertisements in its Monday Media section. However, many people get their first job by word of mouth, by getting a couple of shifts after impressing on a work placement, or by being in the right place at the right time. When you do find a few job advertisements, note down what skills and personal qualities they are looking for. Which elements keep appearing? Do you have the right experience and abilities? If not, what can you do about it?

Yes, radio is competitive. Yes, particularly at the start, the pay can be bad. Yes, the hours are often shocking. But, if this is right for you, a career in radio can be wonderfully fulfilling, great fun and a whole lot better than the average 9 to 5 job. When it is going well, you will pinch yourself that you are getting a wage slip for doing what many people would gladly do for free in their spare time. And do not be put off. The best spur I had was some well-intentioned advice from a university careers adviser to become an accountant, even though I had shown no interest in the subject. 'Why?' I asked. 'It pays well, you got a good mark in maths and radio's impossible to get into.' 'I'll show them', I thought, and – since 1989 – I have been doing just that!

Resources

www.bbc.co.uk – BBC, the biggest of the UK broadcasters and a major employer. Check the jobs section for useful tips.

www.bjtc.org.uk – Broadcast Journalism Training Council – accredits courses in radio, television and online journalism to make sure you learn the skills required by the industry.

www.crca.co.uk – Commercial Radio Companies Association, the trade body for UK commercial radio.

www.commedia.org.uk – Community Media Association, gives access to voices in the community, encouraging creativity and participation.

www.hospitalbroadcasting.co.uk – Hospital Broadcasting Association, supports hospital radio stations across the UK.

www.ofcom.org.uk – OFCOM, the independent regulator and competition authority for, amongst others, the radio industry.

www.skillset.org.uk/radio – Skillset, the skills council for the audio-visual industry in the UK.

www.studentradio.org.uk – Student Radio Association, supports and represents student stations, organising conferences and awards.

ELEVEN Newspaper journalism

The writer of this chapter is Guy Hodgson, a journalist for more than 30 years working for, among others, the Independent *and the BBC. He has been senior lecturer in the Department of Journalism at the University of Central Lancashire since 2000 and still writes regularly on sport for the* Independent on Sunday.

General information

First the good news: if you want to work on a newspaper as journalist, you have an eye for a story and good English skills, the chances are you will get a job. The bad news? You will get a wage considerably lower than graduates entering other professions.

The average starting salary for a graduate is around £19,000; the sort of wage a postgraduate can expect on a weekly newspaper will be £12,500. The National Union of Journalists (NUJ) estimated in January 2006 that a young journalist could lose out by £538,000 over a 44-year career – and their comparison was with university lecturers, who were mounting a campaign themselves to bring themselves into line with other professions (*Journalist*, 2006, January/February: 11–13). The NUJ continued, 'Nearly half of the journalists in the UK earn less than the national average full-time wage of £28,210. More than one in five media workers earn less than the Council of Europe decency threshold of £15,129. Four out of five journalists would be unable as first-time buyers to secure a mortgage to buy the average house in the UK.'

So if money is not the attraction, what is? To contradict the above, the carrot of large wages that can be earned if you make it to the top of the *Sunday Times*, the *Daily Mail* and so on. You meet different and interesting people. The job is unpredictable, and while it has its boring moments it also has excitements that few other professions could match. You are informing and educating the public, exposing injustices or corruption, holding the government to account, and providing entertainment. You may get free tickets for films, theatre and sporting occasions and can travel to exotic locations to see them. And there is the ultimate thrill of seeing your byline in print.

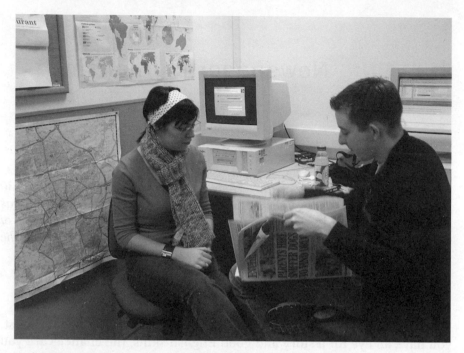

Checking the newspapers is a daily routine for journalists

Those are the cons and pros of being a journalist and you can get there by a variety of routes, but the starting point should be the same. There is no sense hankering for the glamour of the job if you cannot cope with the less appealing parts of it, from interminable lists of results from the flower show to knocking on the door of a grieving widow for a report on an unexpected death. Even a top-level political reporter will have his days when he has to spend hours outside 10 Downing Street waiting for a statement and, lower down the food chain, the final product could be a lot less interesting than the thoughts of the Prime Minister. To put it bluntly, on a local paper you soon find out if you are cut out to be a reporter.

The ideal journalists will have taken an interest in the news from a young age. Be it because they have an interest in sport, celebrity, music and so on, they will have devoured newspapers from their early teens and moved into other sections of the newspaper as their interests have expanded. The best writers usually stem from the most avid readers, and some young journalists have an instinctive nose for the right angle for a story largely because they have spent much of their formative years with that same nose stuck in a newspaper. For them, introductions seem to come naturally.

The way into getting those introductions published has changed over the last 30 years. Once, many young reporters went straight into a job on a local newspaper, often after catching the attention of the senior staff during work experience while they were at school. The wages were as grim in the 1970s as they are now, but, to be fair on the employers, the cost of training journalists fell on newspaper groups. Now, all but the very fortunate few entrants into the industry have already attended a course, either at a university or through the National Council of Training Journalists (NCTJ).

Getting on these courses is not as easy as it may seem. The competition is so strong that applicants need to be able to show they have some commitment to the profession they hope to enter. This usually involves working on school or university magazines and work experience on newspapers, magazines or local radio stations. Certainly, there is no point turning up at an interview for one of these courses with an airy 'I've always wanted to be a writer'. The person sitting opposite you will require some proof.

The best way to get proof is to badger your local newspaper or magazine editor. He or she may get irritated by the 14-year-old who rings up regularly asking for work experience, but only one with an extremely short-sighted view will fail to give credit for persistence. No reporter can thrive without it; editors soon get fed up with young reporters who give up when the first hurdle is placed in their path. Once you get there, do not be satisfied with making the tea and doing errands. In quiet moments ask to shadow a senior reporter on a job. Or ask if you can type up a wedding or football report sent in by a contributor. Keen, able teenagers are soon noted by older journalists, who may be the same people offering jobs when that same youngster seeks employment a few years later. Try to get as many cuttings (copies of your published work) as possible because these will act as proof of your competence when you apply for a course or a job.

Roles in newspaper journalism

What is newspaper journalism exactly? The simple answer is what fills a newspaper, but there are many different roles involved in converting raw news into print. What are those roles?

The most obvious one is that of the general news reporter. He or she will be expected to gather information based around such events as court hearings, council meetings, sporting events and parliament. Those are the predictable 'diary' events. The reporter will also be able to find stories of his or her own by developing their own sources of information, which can vary from an accommodating councillor to the local vicar. In an age of 24-hour news on radio and television, however, a newspaper has to provide something more than just news. Features, often focussing on lifestyle, are increasingly important and these are provided by writers who have usually graduated from general news to develop a specialism.

These are the people who provide the words, the names you see in the bylines, but there is also a large back-up, comprising journalists and executives. These range from the sub-editors, who check and correct the copy provided by the writers, cut it to fill the space designated for it and write a headline, to the page designers and the editors, who are responsible for the look, direction and priorities of the publication.

Skills for newspaper journalism

What skills do newspaper journalists need? Leslie Sellers wrote that the qualities needed in a journalist are so varied that if anyone mastered them all 'he'd stay about a fortnight and then become chairman of Ford or Prime Minister, and we'd all have £100 cars and no income tax' (Sellers, 1982: 10). And Sellers was writing only about sub-editors.

The most obvious skill is an ability to write and recognise good English, but there is so much more to being a good journalist. Knowledge of the law relating to contempt and libel are essential, but then so is good all-round general knowledge. A journalist must be able to work quickly and accurately, often under intense pressure in terms of time. He or she must be able to recognise what will be of interest to the reader and how to enhance that interest by content and design.

Most of all, though, a journalist should have imagination and the drive to put the fruits of that imagination into practice. The best reporters see not just the story, but also the ramifications. He or she hears a story about government reforms to the health service on the radio in the morning and can convert it into a story about the local GP or hospital by the afternoon. Ideas are highly prized commodities in newspapers, and a regular source of them will always be appreciated.

Most editors prefer their young journalists to have passed their seven NCTJ preliminary examinations. The NCTJ's curriculum is under revision, but in 2006/7 the structure is likely to be:

- News writing exam of two hours' duration comprising a news story of 275–325 words, a short story of 70–80 words, a second short story of 40–50 words and follow-up ideas.
- A logbook comprising 10 published cuttings from either work placement or course newspaper pages, one feature and a 500-word feature.

- Public Affairs Part One: four questions on Local Government, one of which is a compulsory finance question.
- Public Affairs Part Two: four questions on Central Government.
- Law Part One: examination of court reporting and related issues in defamation (privilege) and contempt (sections 4 and 11 of the Contempt of Court Act), sources of law, crime terminology and relevant aspects of the Press Complaints Commission (PCC) code.
- Law Part Two: this examines general reporting (excluding court reporting). It will take in defamation, contempt, copyright, confidentiality, other parts of the PCC code.
- Shorthand: 100 words per minute.

Career opportunities

There are 10 national daily newspapers and 11 Sunday nationals in the UK listed in the *Media Directory 2005* (Alden, 2005: 15) (omitting *The Sport* and the *Sunday Sport*). Their circulation varies from 3.3 million for the *News of the World* to 245,000 for *The Independent* (www.abc.org. uk, 2006). Most are based in London, although there are jobs covering regions.

Very few newly qualified reporters get jobs straight on national newspapers, however, and most start on regional or weekly newspapers. The *Media Directory 2005* lists 1,300 newspapers based round the UK with a total circulation of 68.1 million. These are owned by a variety of publishers. Trinity Mirror, Newsquest, Northcliffe and Johnston are the biggest four with 22.9, 15.6, 13.4 and 12.2 per cent of that circulation respectively. The northwest of England has more than 160 titles listed alone, so there should be a newspaper within commuting distance of every aspiring journalist.

Progress and promotion

Because the turnover in staff is high, promotion tends to come quickly and a new journalist can expect to be covering important stories within months, if not weeks, of their arrival on a newspaper. After two years, reporters are usually expected to sit the NCTJ National Certificate Examination, which is designed to examine all-round competence in a range of fundamental skills at a level appropriate to a newspaper journalist who has completed the basic training programme. Pass that and your wages should improve along with your prospects of moving to a better job.

Case study: Nick Owens

Nick Owens is a reporter for the Lancashire Evening Post. *He was voted Young Journalist of the Year 2005 and North West Reporter of the Year 2005.*

What do you do?

'I work as an investigative reporter for the *Lancashire Evening Post* newspaper. This means I spend much of my time working on off-diary news investigations examining issues which affect our readers. I have been doing this since August 2005. This is my first job in the industry.'

How did you get into it? Was it planned or did you happen upon it?

'I got into my job at the *Lancashire Evening Post* after completing a postgraduate diploma in newspaper journalism at the University of Central Lancashire. This was a year-long course and during this time I wrote freelance features for the *Evening Post*. I also went on a two-week work experience placement with the paper and was offered a job at the end of this placement.'

What training did you receive? Do you get more training now?

'The training I received at university was excellent and proved the perfect grounding for my job. I learned about how the law impacts on journalism, about ethical issues which surround the industry. I also learned shorthand and the basic skills of news-writing, the tools needed to search out stories and how a newspaper is laid out and put together. I do get more training now to help with my senior journalism exams – the NCE qualification. This training is a stage on from what I learned at university. I am trained in more legal issues and also given more intensive training about following up stories and creating story ideas each day.'

What are the key skills in your job role?

'For investigations it is important to have a good awareness of the law, be well organised, be tenacious, be willing to take risks, to have an awareness of what your reader is interested in and also, crucially, to be able to digest and handle large amounts of information. These skills, of course, are also vital to all forms of journalism, but the most vital skills for a news reporter are accuracy, being able to work to deadlines and being able to write to length. Often people overlook other skills which can't be taught at university. Good journalists are good with people, are able to show confidence and take control of situations but probably most crucially are good listeners. The best stories come from listening carefully to what people say to you.'

What technical skills are important?

'It is important to have shorthand, to be able to write to a house style, but also to be able to write with flair, to be accurate and thorough and to be able to work well under pressure.'

(Continued)

What are the best and worst aspects of your job?

'It is always satisfying to see your story in print. The day I don't get a buzz from seeing a story of mine bylined in the paper will be the day to get out of the industry. But it is also nice when readers respond to a story you have produced because it shows you are doing your job properly and playing a part within your community, which is what local newspapers in particular should always strive to do. The worse parts of the job are having to do 'death-knocks' – where you have to approach people who have just lost a friend or relative. But often people do want to talk and pay tribute to someone. If they do, it is crucial to get your facts right because often that will be the one chance someone has to pay tribute to someone they have lost.'

What advice would you offer to aspiring newspaper journalists?

'Get out in to your community and be a reporter now. You don't become a journalist when your course ends. Get in people's faces, report on issues happening locally, play a part. This will help you build up your contacts, get a portfolio of work and give you an insight into what it will be like once you start working on a paper.'

What are the key skills for success? How could a person with a film or media degree best approach entry into the career?

'You can be taught a lot but there is also a lot you can't teach. You can't be taught to be enthusiastic, to have good ideas, to show passion and energy. If you can do that you will be 90 per cent of the way there. Journalism is ideas-led. In terms of your training, think about what you might need that perhaps a film or media degree doesn't give you. For instance, could you do a shorthand class in the evening? Could you study media and the law from home?'

How do people get jobs in journalism?

'Often through word of mouth. Many journalists get a job after doing a trial at a newspaper and impressing the managers. Others will get taken on after a period of work experience. Some journalists, who show they have talent, will get poached by other newspapers. It can be difficult to get that first job, but once you have that foot in the door you will soon learn of where other jobs are going.'

What do you see as the future of this work?

'Journalism at a local level is going to have to change in the next years. Local papers are struggling to increase sales, and I think more and more emphasis will be placed on the Internet. More readers now use the net to access local news and newspapers and local journalists will have to learn

(Continued)

(Continued)

new skills to supply the service a rising number of people now demand. Newspapers will never die because they still have a vital role to play in communities, but it would be naive to think the Internet will not provide a great challenge to the print media, because it will.'

What about your own future? What are your ambitions?

'I want to continue learning and continue improving as a journalist. If that leads me on to a better and bigger role in the industry, then so be it. I would like to work on a national newspaper one day, but perhaps move back in to local newspapers at a slightly higher level. What I like about local newspapers is they can still set agendas and make a difference within their community. That is a satisfying thing to be involved in.'

Case study: Ella Stimson

Ella Stimson is a researcher/editorial assistant for The Times.

What is your role?

'I am a researcher/editorial assistant on the features section of *The Times* (*Times2*). My job mainly involves researching stories, arranging interviews, and writing and interviewing, generally for case studies, boxes and side-bars to accompany features. I have been doing this job since May 2005, and it is my first job in the newspaper industry.'

How did you get that first break?

'I originally went to the features desk to do work experience in 2003 after graduating from university where I studied English. In 2005 I returned to do more work experience as part of a postgraduate journalism course. When I finished the placement, they asked me if I wanted to return when I completed the course, and I worked there for two months before I started to get paid full-time. During this time I also did work experience placements on the foreign desk at *The Times* and the foreign desk at the *Sunday Times*.'

What kind of training has been useful to you?

'I did a postgraduate diploma in newspaper journalism which covered all aspects of the newspaper industry, including ethics, law and politics, and was an excellent preparation for my current job.'

What skills do you need in your current role?

'The most crucial skills are being able to work under pressure, meet deadlines without compromising accuracy, being able to work to a brief and

(Continued)

write to set length. I need to be able to absorb large amounts of information in a short space of time and extract the essential points. Finally, it is important to be persuasive, which comes from having confidence in yourself and being as well-informed as possible on the subject at hand. Whoever you are dealing with, you need to be able to win their trust and convince them to talk to you.'

Do you use any technical skills?

'Shorthand has been a lifesaver – there are many occasions when I do quick telephone interviews and there just isn't time to record and transcribe them. It is well worth the hours of practice it takes to master.'

What do you like best about your role, and what least?

'I love the variety it offers – there is no typical day. The range of stories we cover means I could work on something very serious and news-based in the morning, and then spend the afternoon talking to celebrities' agents. I have also done things like fixing interviews, dealing with book extracts, conducting vox pops and collaborating on pieces with other writers. It has been fantastic to be in a position where I can build up such a wide range of experience. Of course, there is also the buzz of seeing something you have written in the paper, and of seeing the finished product come off the press and knowing that you have made a contribution, however small! The only downside is probably the pressure – it can get very intense as deadlines approach, and if you need to stay late, come in early or work on bank holidays, there is no way round it.'

What advice would you offer to students and graduates who want to follow your footsteps?

'They should certainly give serious consideration to some kind of formal journalistic training, particularly a postgraduate course. They give you a solid grounding in the skills you need and are very well-respected in the industry. Even if you want to work in features or magazines, it will stand you in good stead. It is probably not an entry requirement for my current job, but it certainly has helped, and I know that having that qualification means other opportunities will be open to me along the way. At the very least, it has given me confidence that I am up to the job and I know what I'm doing.'

How could a graduate of film or media best approach entry into a role like yours?

'Be keen and committed. Getting a foot in the door is so important, and you might have to undertake a few thankless tasks to get there. Approach

(Continued)

(Continued)

as many papers and magazines as you can asking for work, even if it is part-time or unpaid. Make the most of any work or work experience you get. If you are enthusiastic, full of ideas and prepared to work hard, people will remember you.'

How do people get jobs in journalism?

'There are many, many routes, so don't confine your job search to advertised vacancies. A lot of jobs are filled through word of mouth, which is why it is so important to start making contacts. If you are doing part-time work or work experience, you will be in a much better position to hear about vacancies, and if a job comes up, people may think of you. Whatever role you are aiming for, it will be much easier to get there from the inside of the industry than the outside.'

What are your hopes for the future?

'I want to make the most of the opportunities I have, get as much experience as possible, and write more. Ultimately I would like to be a feature writer, but I am well aware that news experience is a massive advantage, and I would like to spend time working in a newsroom at some point.'

Resources

References

Alden, Chris (ed.) (2005) *Media Directory 2005*. London: Guardian Books.
National Union of Journalists (2006) *The Missing Half Million*, research by David Ayrton, Journalist. London: NUJ.
Sellers, Leslie (1982) *The Simple Subs Book*. Oxford: Pergamon.

Website reference

www.abc.org.uk – ABC, (accessed 6 June 2007), average circulation, 2 April 2007 to 29 April 2007.

Useful books

Adams, S. and Hicks, W. (2001) *Interviewing for Journalists*. London: Routledge.
Frost, C. (2002) *Reporting for Journalists*. London: Routledge.
Hennessy, B. (2006) *Writing Feature Articles*. Oxford: Elsevier.
Hicks, W. (1998) *English for Journalists*. London: Routledge.
Hicks, W. (1998) *Writing for Journalists*. London: Routledge.
Hicks, W. and Holmes, T. (2002) *Subediting for Journalists*. London: Routledge.

Useful websites

www.nuj.org.uk – The National Union of Journalists.

www.nctj.com – The training body for the British print media.

www.pressgazette.co.uk – The weekly journal of the media industry.

www.newsdesk-uk.com and www.journalism.co.uk – Independent websites for media professionals.

TWELVE   Magazine journalism

This chapter is written by Cathy Darby, Course Leader for the Masters in Magazine Journalism at the University of Central Lancashire. Before she joined the department, Cathy was a news sub-editor on the Lancashire Evening Post. *Previously she was a sub-editor at the* Daily Mail, *a surveys editor at the* Financial Times *and chief sub-editor of* Country Life.

Getting into magazine journalism

You want to be a magazine journalist? Is it the thought of rubbing shoulders with celebrities? Attending film premieres? Reviewing upcoming bands? Test driving the latest 4 × 4? Sampling spas? Interviewing stars? Well, yes, magazine journalism can offer perks such as these, but be warned: the competition to land jobs in the industry is intense, and is set to become even fiercer. Why? Because with over 8,000 titles on offer and consumer spending topping the £2 billion mark for the first time ever in 2004, magazines are currently the success story of the print industry. And British magazines are the best in the world. As Colin Kennedy, film magazine *Empire*'s editor and publisher, said recently, 'if you can make it here, you make it anywhere' (Kennedy, 2006).

That's the rub, though. How do you make it in an industry where 98 per cent are graduates and 70 per cent are under 40? It's not just a question of having a degree, lots of ambition and an interest in creative writing. How do you make it in an industry which is happy to keep wannabes on extended unpaid work placements in the hopes of landing that first job as an editorial assistant? Which means deep pockets, a lot of debt or depending upon the Bank of Mummy and Daddy – not an option open to many? How do you make it in an industry which still relies so much on the old boy or, just as much, old girl network to give you that essential contact with potential employers? And if it's so difficult to get a foothold in the industry, why is magazine journalism so popular?

Because, as with newspaper journalism, few other professions can match it for its creative satisfaction and the ultimate high of seeing your name in print either as a byline or in the staff box. It's not a job for clock-watchers – unless it is to look up suddenly and wonder where the morning has gone. Or even, with a deadline looming, wishing you could turn the clock back. It is a job for those who love a challenge and thrive under pressure.

What is the difference between newspapers and magazines? Isn't magazine journalism all about fashion and lifestyle, the frothy stuff? Indeed not. While newspapers are a broad church embracing a host of different interests to attract as wide an audience as possible, magazines, and supplements within newspapers, are much more targeted. They focus on a particular area of interest – travel, fashion, health, business or, in business magazines (B2Bs), the business itself of travel, fashion or health. Magazines' core strength is creating and serving a community of readers to whom they deliver trusted copy with high editorial standards and levels of creativity. When you open the pages of a successful magazine you should step into a club of mutual interests, whether it's fly fishing, frocks or politics.

This doesn't mean magazines aren't newsworthy. Quite the opposite. Celebrity magazines break stories about stars and newspapers often reprint interviews originally given to glossies. Health journals deliver scoops on latest medical advances and research, and the trade press breaks stories in their fields of expertise. From computers to music, magazines regularly set the agenda as the source of news for all other media. So it's even more important to have new information, but targeted to your particular readership's interests, for a flourishing relationship and healthy circulation.

According to broadcaster and publisher Andrew Neil, former editor of the *Sunday Times* and founding chairman of Sky TV, technology has led to daily newspapers increasingly being overlooked, particularly by a younger generation, in favour of the Internet. Print still has power and efficacy, he says, however, through 'features, analysis, comment, story and pictures – all core strengths of magazines' (www.fipp.com, accessed 30 March 2006).

This is why those who want to write for magazines and newspapers must first acquire research, news- and feature-writing skills. Using the example given in the previous chapter, a reporter who hears a story about government reforms to the health service on the radio in the morning can convert it into a story about the local GP or hospital by the afternoon. For a magazine journalist, a story must be written for a particular market. So a writer on a doctor's magazine, such as *GP*, the news of government health reforms might prompt an idea for a feature on how it would affect GPs as a profession. A writer for *Mother and Baby* would focus on how such reforms would affect families.

As a magazine journalist you must be a lateral thinker, a self-starter and capable of spotting ideas that could be developed into features.

A great deal of time is spent in planning and preparation

After a number of years' experience, building contacts and expertise, some journalists may choose to freelance. The dream of many, it is the lifestyle of the fortunate, well-connected and hard-working few who have learnt the disciplines of writing to order.

Roles in magazine journalism

The primary role is that of a reporter or writer. However, the number of full-time staff journalists varies enormously from one magazine to another. Some current affairs magazines may list a large number of names of staff writers. At the other extreme, a skeleton editorial team will be supplemented by freelance writers and photographers and casual sub-editors brought in close to edition times. On tighter teams, writers may also double up as sub-editors. On the tightest of teams, the features editor, chief sub-editor and editor may well be one and the same person.

Sub-editors are the safety net for journalists – and editors. They check and correct copy according to legal requirements and the publication's house style, cut it to fit the space available and write the accompanying headlines, captions and standfirsts (the paragraph that usually sums up a feature and includes the author's byline) and checking whether the corrections have been made in the final proofs. A good sub-editor should have an understanding of the principles of page design and knowledge of QuarkXpress and/or InDesign in packaging the publication for its target market.

Skills and training for magazine journalism

The first and pre-eminent requirement is the ability to write and recognise good English. Research skills are valuable not just for developing copy, but also to check it for accuracy. Magazine journalists must have good general knowledge and magpie alertness to fresh story ideas. They need to be creative and lateral thinkers, capable of developing and packaging new ideas for their target market.

As with the newspaper industry, most magazine editors prefer to see applicants who do not require further training. They are happy to consider candidates from courses accredited by the Periodicals Training Council (PTC), which only gives its blessing to those organisations that produce journalists with the skills sought by magazine employers.

Work experience is an excellent way to get a foot in the industry door. The PTC's parent organisation, the Periodicals Publishing Association (PPA), the trade association for British magazines, lists tips to get your application into the top 2 per cent. You need to prove your worth to potential editors, bringing skills and problem-solving experience to lighten their load. The final tip says 'in an editor's dream you write like an angel; have a rock solid, news-based qualification and have been passionate about the subject since you were knee-high to a spotty toadstool. In practice, any two of these three will probably get you an interview.' (www.ppa.co.uk, accessed 30 March 2006).

The National Council for the Training of Journalists (NCTJ) runs and accredits magazine courses on which it offers a Magazine Certificate.

The sector

According to the PPA, the 3,324 current consumer magazines are those which provide leisure-time information and entertainment, from *Heat* to *FHM*, while business or B2B magazines, formerly the trade press, from *The Stage* to *Farmers' Weekly*, account for 5,142. These are produced by well-established creative publishing houses, Emap, Condé Nast, IPC, Hachette-Filipacchi, and enterprising newcomers such as the customer publisher August Media, founded in 2005, which produces the magazine for IKEA in 10 languages with a print run of 1.7 million.

The newest arrivals to the periodicals market are such customer magazines which have seen 127 per cent rise in turnover since 1995, with a total value of £366 million. These are produced by publishers such as Haymarket, Redwood and August under contract for companies and distributed free or offered for sale to customers. The most notable example is *Sky* magazine, with the magazine industry's biggest circulation overall at 5.18 million, which dwarfs that of the more popular magazine image of *Glamour* at 609,626 and even the leading consumer paid-for *What's On TV* at 1.67 million. The advertisers' bible *Brad* (Brad Online is available by subscription on the Internet at www.intellagencia.com) lists the UK's magazines' details including their target market and circulation.

Magazines have a better starting salary compared to newspapers. Many of the jobs are based in the southeast of England around the capital, although the regions are beginning to launch new magazines and periodicals. Unlike the huge infrastructure needed to publish a newspaper, the dynamism of the sector is driven by desktop publishing, which allows magazines to be published anywhere with access to a PC and a local printer.

Once on board a magazine, progress can be rapid as the unfortunate side of this dynamic industry is the speed with which magazines flourish or sink if they fail to reach or misunderstand their target market. Age is no protector, as with the demise of Emap's 28-year-old *Smash Hits* in February 2006. What appears to be a drawback, however, is a given within the profession and often opens doors to new opportunities, especially to a journalist with bright, original ideas which are gold dust in an industry that's hungry for copy.

Case study: Amy Carroll

Amy Carroll is sub-editor at Essential Publishing for REAL magazine and also editor of the REAL Talks Sex page.

Can you tell us what you do?

'It's a really varied job. In my sub-editor role, most of my time is devoted to getting copy into a fit state to go in the magazine, working with the picture editor and designer, writing the contents pages and writing straplines for the cover. When the dummy book is complete, I also sit down with the other sub-editor and we proof the whole thing. I also commission features, call in products and commission images for the *REAL* Talks Sex page. I chat to PR [public relations] companies and research new launches.'

How did you land it? Was it what you planned?

'With persistence! I had found the company when doing a search of publishing houses and instantly knew that I wanted to get a job on *REAL*. I sent

(Continued)

my CV and a letter in a silver envelope in March, sent the Director an email to alert him to the arrival of a silver envelope and, after not hearing back and never having my emails returned, I emailed him again to ask if he would like me to stop calling. He phoned me instantly, chatted to me for 20 minutes and agreed to me coming in to do work experience for two weeks. At first I worked on *TVHits*, but then I was invited back to do a week of subbing on *REAL*. I got my job in August, and only after a lot of calls and effort!'

What training did you need to get the job?

'I needed to have passed exams in law and had to demonstrate that I was reliable. They seemed most concerned about this aspect. I think that my week's experience here was more important than my qualifications, but having an MA and NCTJ qualifications certainly helped me fast-track. I think that it gave me credibility when I had minimal experience.'

What are the key skills in your job role?

'Subbing, proofing, writing, multi-tasking, organisation, forward planning, flexibility, research skills, persuasion! I have to be able to respond to last-minute changes in flatplans and without showing any signs of being flustered!'

What technical skills are important?

'It has been essential to be confident with QuarkXpress because I spend half of my time proofing on screen and moving boxes around etc. Without understanding the basics of Quark, I'd be much slower. InDesign skills are the next thing to learn, though. We work on Macs here, and although I had never used one before I quickly adjusted.'

What are the most satisfying aspects of the work? What are the worst?

'The highs are working with a great team, seeing raw copy – often full of mistakes and badly written – transformed into attractive features. I enjoy the creative input and the opportunity to work with writers, designers and also with the editor. As a sub, I get some input at most stages of the production cycle. The worst thing about my job? When you write good headlines or straps and they don't get used! Dealing with features that haven't been commissioned properly, cleaning up after a breakdown in communication. But even the downsides aren't that bad.'

What advice would you offer to aspiring magazine journalists?

'Arm yourself with ideas. Keep an eye on what's going on in competing magazines and always have a suggestion up your sleeve. Don't assume that everyone in senior positions knows more than you do, but don't be too pushy. Be enthusiastic, prepared to work late and always hand in clean copy.'

(Continued)

(Continued)

What are the key skills for success?

'I found that everything covered by my MA in Magazine Journalism equipped me for a successful career. When I went on my first work experience placement, I was already up to speed and able to write, research, contribute to creative planning and, most of all, I understood the bigger picture. In magazine journalism, you have to acquire the skills necessary, but you also have to understand the relationship between advertising and editorial needs, editorial values and the concerns that a publishing director will have. So, it's not just about skills.'

How do people get jobs in magazine journalism?

'Be persistent. There are more people than there are jobs and even when you apply for something there's probably someone who's just been in for work experience the week before. You have to be prepared to go and impress, not just send your CV.'

What do you see as the future of the magazine industry?

'I think that we are seeing more and more magazines starting up, so it's obviously a growing industry. Perhaps magazines will have their core staff in the office, but freelancers will be used for writing most of the copy.'

What about your own future? What are your ambitions?

'I have been in my first job for six months and have just secured a promotion. I'm going from consumer to customer-based, but will be working on a new launch at Redwood Publishing. I actually met my new editor through the Masters course that I did. I arranged to shadow her for a week and took part in the creative planning of the Marks & Spencer magazine that she edited. Based on this work experience, and keeping in touch with her, I now find myself going to join her team. I think that the most important thing is to be working with creative, experienced colleagues who are going to get the best out of you. I also wanted to work for a company that values training and professional development. What kind of magazine you actually work for isn't that important in terms of career progression. Finding a mentor, someone you respect, is probably more important.'

Case study: *Chris Wood is a reporter for* Materials Recycling Weekly *at Emap.*

What is your job?

Reporter for *Materials Recycling Week* (*MRW*).

(Continued)

Can you describe what you do?

'Write up press releases, phone contacts and industry officials trying to find stories, look through the Internet/newspapers for stories and attend industry meetings/announcements/awards etc.

How did you land it? Was it what you planned?

'It was not planned. As I completed my Magazine Journalism Masters in July 2005, my tutor sent me through a number of job advertisements and I applied to three or four of them on a random basis. *MRW* was the only one of these to offer me an interview and then a second interview. I think the variety of skills (such as the MA, shorthand, subbing, news-writing) on my CV helped me gain an interview. And obviously, at an interview stage, it all depends if they like you and how suitable they feel you are for the position. As *MRW* was looking for a young, aspiring journalist (primarily because they are 'cheaper' than hiring someone with more experience), I seemed to fit the bill.'

What training did you need to get the job?

'At interview, the shorthand qualification seemed to be a big plus, while the NCTJ news-writing skills were also essential as the job entails a high level of news-story writing. Also, a higher degree in a journalistic discipline was vital to securing the role.'

Do you get more training now?

'I have been given more training on using the computer system we use, while further news-writing/feature-writing training is also available to me, as is training in a variety of domains from management skills to foreign languages!'

What are the key skills in your job role?

'The key skills are communication, being able to talk and uncover stories. Also, being able to find newsworthy elements or angles on information or dialogue which may not initially seem that interesting. Being able to supply a constant stream of stories and, when they are not instantly available, being able to find them.'

What technical skills are important?

'The ability to form the structure of stories, be it news story or feature, and write in a manner appropriate for the target audience. Developing news-writing skills and a knowledge and understanding of a live website. With

(Continued)

(Continued)

this updated daily, putting in stories and keeping it updated is another important element of the job, as well as an ability to use Word documents and the Internet as a resource.'

What are the most satisfying aspects of the work? What are the worst?

'The most satisfying parts are gaining an exclusive story – one that you have worked on and are the first to publish. Lows are the monotony of working for an industry magazine that at times can seem quite boring and mundane. In any job there are good times and bad times, but the work is fairly relaxed, I have got pretty much a free rein to work on what I want – as long as I get the right amount of stories produced, my boss is satisfied. So, the freedom is certainly a plus, but occasionally the recycling industry does bore me slightly!'

What advice would you offer to aspiring magazine journalists?

'I think you've got to be prepared to start at the bottom and work your way up. There is no quick fix in journalism (unless you're extremely fortunate or talented). In a perfect world, I don't think anybody on my current publication would be where they are now, but experience is everything in journalism and without it even the most qualified is nothing. So, I think you must first accept that you are going to most probably start somewhere on not very much money and doing something you don't necessarily like. But a journalist must also be alert. There is a lot of opportunity out there so as long as you are constantly thinking one step ahead, looking at other opportunities, you will always progress.'

What are the key skills for success?

'Open-mindedness, an ability to fit in to different situations and a dedication to the cause, realising that it will take a number of years before you have got to where you really want to be. Obviously, you must have an ability to write, but of more importance is being able to apply this to different situations and publications, knowing what style to adopt and when.'

How do people get jobs in magazine/online journalism?

'I think you just need to send your CV to as many people as you can. You can do no more than get qualifications, then after that it is how you present yourself on your CV, with skills learnt on a course and relevant work experience. The better your applications, the more chance of getting an interview. Then at that stage, it is about convincing the potential employer that you are keen, ambitious and ready to become a journalist.'

What do you see as the future of the magazine industry?

'Consumerism continues to grow and, as with everything else, people are going to purchase magazines in increased quantities. There are more and

(Continued)

more titles springing up all the time and publications taking new angles on older concepts. The magazine industry has to be the boom sector in journalism as it is able to exist in so many different formats.'

What about your own future? What are your ambitions?

'I intend to stay in my current job for a year and then after that will review the situation. I am ambitious to write for a consumer magazine, and be given a freer rein to develop features and stories on topics that are more interesting, such as travel, sport, cinema, current affairs, television and so on. But I believe a year at this position will give me a grounding to move on to the next level. I will submit pieces to various magazines as well to gain other marks on my CV, but at the moment I consider myself to be in the early stages of my development, with still a fair bit to learn.'

Resources

References

Kennedy, C. (2006) Periodical Training Council forum, London: 9 March.
Neil, A. (2006) www.fipp.com, accessed 30 March.
Periodicals Publishing Association (2006) www.ppa.co.uk, accessed 30 March.

Useful books

Adams, S. and Hicks, W. (2001) *Interviewing for Journalists*. London: Routledge.
Frost, C. (2002) *Reporting for Journalists*. London: Routledge.
Hennessy, B. (2006) *Writing Feature Articles*. Oxford: Elsevier.
Hicks, W. (1998) *English for Journalists*. London: Routledge.
Hicks, W. (1998) *Writing for Journalists*. London: Routledge.
Hicks, W. and Holmes, T. (2002) *Subediting for Journalists*. London: Routledge.
Hoffman, A. (1999) *Research for Writers*. London: A & C Black.
MacKay, J (2006) *The Magazines Handbook*. London: Routledge.
Morrish, J. (2003) *Magazine Editing*. London: Routledge.

Useful websites

www.ppa.co.uk – The Periodicals Publishing Association, the trade association for the British magazine industry, includes a website directory of the 400 companies currently in membership, representing around 2,3000 consumer, business and professional magazines.

www.nctj.com – The National Council for the Training of Journalists, the training body for the British print media.

www.pressgazette.co.uk – The weekly journal of the media industry.

www.newsdesk-uk.com and www.journalism.co.uk – Independent websites for media professionals.

THIRTEEN Publishing

The author of this section is Michaela Schoop, who has wide experience of the publishing industry. She gained a Postgraduate Certificate in Printing and Publishing from the London College of Printing and Publishing. She started her career as a reprint controller at publisher Chapman & Hall, then worked as a production controller at academic publisher Routledge, with special responsibilities for architecture and civil engineering books. After

Michaela Schoop

this she became a senior production controller for children's book specialist Egmont, focusing on baby and novelty books.

Publishing industry overview

Despite all the technological and digital advances, the printed word is still prolifically produced and consumed. Publishing is a growth industry with a bright future ahead. Currently, the UK publishing industry, including newspapers, magazines and business-to-business publishing, is estimated to have a total value of more than £22 billion and employs 194,000 people. There are over 9,850 establishments in the publishing sector, of which 30 per cent are book publishers. The UK book and journal publishing industry is the second largest in Europe and alone accounts for a £4.5 billion turnover employing 36,000 people.

Publishing companies require a set of skills and core competencies consisting of acquisition, selection, editing, management, marketing and sale of content. Consequently, this dynamic industry is in need of people with varied skills, and it offers them a variety of exciting job opportunities.

As a recent graduate, what do you need to know and what do you need to do to get into publishing? First, you need to be aware that there are many different areas in the publishing industry:

- books
- magazines and newspapers
- journals and periodicals
- electronic publishing, for example online text books
- mixed media publishing, for example cd/tape with book
- publishing for commercial companies for example, promotional material and internal publishing, for charities and other not-for-profit sectors.

Some companies specialise in one of the above fields, while others may cover a range of them.

Traditional publishing houses can be further broken down into the different publishing markets they specialise in, such as:

- General or Trade: fiction, non-fiction, illustrated books such as cook books, so-called coffee table books and children's books
- Academic: text books
- Science Technical and Medical (STM)
- Business/Professional, for example management, law publishers
- Reference, such as dictionaries, often mixed media and electronic
- Educational, including language books.

Again, specialisms are not necessarily exclusive. For example, an academic publisher may produce a limited number of a paper-printed journal in addition to their main commercial online publication. The bigger the company, the more likely you are to find them working in more than one area. In order to publish their content, publishers utilise a variety of platforms such as the printed word, online publishing, CD-ROMs, e-books and even mobile phones. A lot of the time the content gets repackaged, for example a children's story is released as a paperback, a hardback, a board book edition, as part of a collection, as well as being published as part of a magazine and parts used for an online website. In some cases only the images get re-used, as they are time-consuming and expensive to produce, and they are paired with new or edited text.

For a first job it is worth passing by the large companies and consider finding out and working for a small publishing house: 88 per cent of the book publishing companies have less than 10 employees and 96 per cent employ less than 50 people. There are only 30 book publishing companies who employ 150 or more. Tony Moore, senior commissioning editor for Taylor & Francis, advises new graduates to look for market leaders in their fields, not necessarily the big, household publishing names.

Don't ignore the less glamorous areas of the business. Specialist publishers may make more money, may provide stronger job security and may even be better run. Quantity does not necessary spell profits. The large trade publishers very often operate on much smaller unit profit margins than smaller, more specialised companies. In trade publishing 20 per cent of publishers' titles account for 80 per cent of their revenues, whilst fewer than 40 publishers account for 56 per cent of bookshop sales.

Publishing is a very competitive business. Many publishers compete for sales in the same market. Not only do publishers measure their success in terms of profit, but also in terms of market share, that is, their relative position in sales against other publishers' sales. The aim of the larger publishing houses is to grow both in profit and market share. One way they do it is by buying or merging companies. This happens all the time, and many small companies get swallowed by the larger ones. Thus many well-known imprints, which used to be independent book publishers, are now part of a large publishing group, such as Penguin Books and DK now being part of the Pearson Group. Also larger companies may sell off parts of their business to get rid of areas which do not fit into their business plan.

Pros and cons of working in publishing

Publishing can be both challenging and rewarding, nerve-wracking and exciting. But holding the finished product of your work and seeing it in the bookshops at the end is very satisfying. You have a real sense of ownership. Fast turnover of staff means that you can change your job fairly frequently as positions become available. However, this flexibility is regionally limited.

The workplace is very often relatively informal as the workforce is relatively young (averaging the late-twenties to mid-thirties). And, yes, it is no myth, in general you do tend to work with very nice people.

It is a changing industry which is affected by technological advances, so you will always have to learn new skills. This keeps it interesting but can also be a disadvantage as it can be difficult to get back into work after a lengthy break. Employment opens up possibilities for freelance work and working from home.

Wages are fairly low: currently the average graduate starting salary is about £15,000. The average salary in the business is about £22,500.

The geographical area of employment is strongly polarised. According to regional data, 64 per cent of all book publishing employment is in London and the southeast, compared with 48 per cent of all publishing employment. It is an area of low job security – mergers, sell-offs and acquisition of companies can mean restructuring and redundancies. Most employees have to face the threat of redundancy at least once during their career.

Roles within publishing

It is useful, whichever type of publishing you want to enter, to be aware of the complete publishing process. Not only will it make you seem knowledgeable at your interview, but it will also help you immensely once you start working.

In book publishing, in a very simplistic form, each book goes through three processes:

1. **Origination**: An author submits text for consideration of publishing or an editor commissions an author to write text. The text gets checked for content quality and saleability.
2. **Production**: The book gets proofread, edited, designed and manufactured.
3. **Delivery**: The book gets delivered to a warehouse and then sold on to retail and distribution outlets, or a book gets delivered directly to a customer.

In addition there are the marketing, sales and rights departments and a whole host of administrative jobs that keep a company running, such as personnel, accounts, IT and other administration. You need to know that every publishing house has a slightly different structure and job titles may vary considerably.

Generally, the bigger the company, the more specialised the jobs are, and you can gain an in-depth knowledge of your particular field of employment. However, Tony Moore, Senior Editor at Taylor & Francis, with whom I used to work advises: 'Small publishers are easier to get into and better places to start out as you see the whole of the business more readily'. Thus a small company with a limited number of staff needs their employees to take on a variety of different jobs, that is, a commissioning editor may also have to proofread and do part of the marketing. This enables you to gain knowledge in many different publishing areas but maybe not as in-depth as in a larger company. Working for a small publisher is often a very good way to get started and, once you have gained a wide knowledge of aspects of publishing, you can move on into your second job and specialise in your preferred area.

Consider applying for a job in a subject area you may find unexciting but have the necessary skills to gain entry in. Once you have gained the relevant work experience you often can cross over into your preferred area of publishing as most publishing skills are transferable. People move from journals or magazines to books and from books to electronic media.

Listed below are some of the most common categories of jobs in publishing.

A commissioning editor

Establishes and maintains author contact and gets them to write a book or series of books for the publishing house. Editors manage both the front list, (the output of new books) as well as looking after the back list (books that have been in publication for some time and may need to be reprinted or be allowed to go out of print). A commissioning editor relies on his or her contacts with authors and needs to be aware of trends and developments in their area of publication to recognise demand. This is the job with the highest profile in publishing.

However, unless you are very, very lucky and have rare specialist subject knowledge, your first graduate job will not be a commissioning editor. Even a job as an editorial assistant, who in reality concern themselves initially with very menial tasks and are glorified secretaries, is competitive and hard to come by because of the perceived glamour of commissioning. To get an editorial assistant's job you should have basic keyboard skills (touch-typing is a definite advantage), be highly literate and have good interpersonal skills.

A production editor

Oversees the process from manuscript to the finished book, or at least until hand-over of finished designed typescript on disk to the production team. Generally, this is mostly a project managerial role, but may also include some editing and proofreading. It is important to be able to spell, and very often you need to do very basic proofreading checks, even if the majority may be outsourced.

It depends very much on the company you work for how many different computer software programmes you need to know. Some only require basic knowledge of email and word processing packages, while others may have use of specialist page makeup programmes such as, for example, Quark Xpress or InDesign.

A copy-editor

Gets most deeply involved with the actual content of a book. He or she reads the entire book, checks that quotes are correct, ensures that no gross content mistakes or libellous passages are in the book, may mark up the manuscript, check that pictures are referenced and that house style is followed correctly. Publishing uses a standardised system to correct and mark up typescripts. It is very useful for editorial and production staff, but essential for copy-editors to know how do this. Get hold of a copy and learn them,[1] or better still, take a short course offered by a training organisation that is recognised by the industry. Many companies use freelancers to do copy-editing work. If you make the right connections you may be able to gain experience as a freelancer before getting employment. However, freelancers mostly are people who move out of full-time employment in publishing and build on their acquired skills.

A production or manufacturing controller

Sees through the manufacturing from disk to printed book delivered into the warehouse. In order to do this job you need strong project management and numeracy skills. It is one of the most technical jobs in publishing, and you need to know the processes that go into producing a book. Technological developments mean the production processes change constantly and it is essential to keep up-to-date with these changes. Production controllers very often help develop book formats along with design and editorial staff. They are responsible for creating work schedules and, as they are at the end of the production process, need to chase both editorial and design teams to implement these. Generally, up to two-thirds of the cost spent on a book is spent by the production department. They source printers, get estimates and control cost throughout production. It is their job to check the quality of the end product and ensure delivery to the warehouse or customer.

A designer

Is responsible for translating the editor's and marketing ideas into a text and cover design. Very often they commission artwork for covers from a freelance designer, artist or photographer. Designers nearly always have a design degree and need to be able to work with special design software such as Illustrator, Photoshop and QuarkXpress.

---

[1] The British Standards of proof marks can be bought online at www.bsi-global.com/bsonline, alternatively, invest in Judith Butcher's *Copy Editing*, the copy-editor's bible.

Contacting people by telephone is likely to be a major part of the job

Sales representatives

Are employed by the larger publishing houses. Each sales rep. will have built up personal relationship with customers, which is the most important part of the job.

With increasing globalisation of markets, export or international sales is of growing importance. Reps tend to sell either English books into foreign markets or find customers for foreign language co-editions. Language skills are a definite advantage for an international sales executive. Luckily, English is the international sales language at book fairs, however, it does make transactions a lot smoother if you speak the customers' language and are aware of cultural differences in etiquette. You also need very good personal skills.

Marketing and publicity

Roles, depending of the sort of books you sell, for example science books or children's books, can be very varied. You may get involved in the production of catalogues, press releases, representing the company with products at conferences and fairs, come up with special promotional offers and commission special point-of-sale displays. It is an advantage to have sales experience, so consider working for a bookshop or even a library, or in the marketing department of another kind of company.

The licensing or rights department

Deals with secure licensing and publishing rights. The acquisition of licensing and publishing rights can be very competitive as, once you have acquired the rights to a well-known brand or product, there is a lot of money to be spent, but also made, in particular if this is tied in with a popular television or movie series such as, for example, *Star Wars* or *Harry Potter*.

Publishing services

Are responsible for stock control. They ensure that there are enough copies of key titles in the warehouse to satisfy customer demand. At the same time, they see that the warehouse, which charges the publishers for stock held, does not carry slow sellers for too long. Non-sellers are either sold off cheaply to special discount stores or get pulped. In order to be good at this job you have to be meticulous, like order, systems and processes, and be helpful and able to communicate at all levels. You need to be familiar with spreadsheet programmes such as Excel. You will probably be trained in other specialist stock monitoring packages.

Freelance opportunities

Publishing uses many freelancers, working both in- or out-house as proofreaders, picture researchers, illustrators and copy-editors. One reason for this is to keep overheads low. On the other hand, certain jobs are so specialised that their services may be needed only once a year or so.

Job titles are not entirely consistent across publishing houses and the responsibilities may vary considerably. A production editor at one company may have very different responsibilities to a production editor at another company, and some companies may not even have anyone employed under this job title. The same applies for the hierarchical naming of job titles. Not all the lower-level job titles, such as assistants or juniors, may be found in a publishing house. Some companies may omit these titles but start people off as, for example, editors. In effect they are still assistants or juniors, this is just not reflected by their job titles.

Getting into publishing

It can be difficult to get into this industry. It has a glamorous reputation and you will probably face stiff competition, especially at entry level.

The most popular and oversubscribed areas are fiction, children's books and high-profile publishing companies. Consider targeting science, technical and medical (STM) or academic publishing. Keep an open mind what role to aim for. Don't limit yourself to editorial. In large general publishing companies, as many as 30 per cent of vacancies can be production related, while less than 10 per cent of job applicants are interested in this area. By contrast, the 10 per cent of vacancies that are for editorial positions attract 50 per cent of applicants (*Bookseller*, 2002, www.thebookseller.com). Expect to start at the very bottom. Don't think that because you have a degree you will be out of place starting in such 'lowly' positions such as secretary or receptionist. Publishing has a very highly educated workforce. In addition to having a degree, many publishers look for some form of publishing experience from a first-time job applicant.

It is well worth attending a specialist publishing training course. There are a variety of postgraduate courses and short courses available. Many employers see these courses as basic training grounds, which also show your commitment to publishing. A postgraduate course in printing and publishing at the London College of Communication is invaluable, in particular for production and manufacturing job seekers.

Consider doing work experience. Use it to gain industry knowledge and to get to know people. It is mostly unpaid but, if you are lucky, travel expenses may be paid. Don't stay anywhere too long without being paid. You are not there to be exploited. But you may find out about a job within that company, and generally applications for internal appointments/promotion are encouraged. Gain commercial awareness by working in a bookshop. Teaching experience can be an advantage to getting children's books and educational jobs. Freelancing can be a way in, but you need some experience as they will not train you. Spend your time improving your skills in typing, IT and proofreading.

Finding out about available jobs

Nationally, publishers mainly advertise in the *Bookseller* (published on Fridays) or the *Media Guardian* (Monday editions), some at junior but mostly at more senior level. Check out their job pages or their websites on the relevant days. Outside of London it is worth looking at local newspapers. Many publishers choose to recruit through their own websites, and the Internet is seen as a useful option. Some publishers advertise via message boards at specialist colleges, especially first time jobs – this way their search is efficiently targeted and it is cheaper than via a newspaper.

Word of mouth both within a company and between companies is one of the most popular ways of finding new staff. For instance, you may be turned down for a job, but your details may be passed on to another publisher. Never forget that publishing is a small community. People move around and you never know where and in what position you will encounter them again.

For your first job, consider signing up with an employment agency which specialises in recruiting secretarial and administrative staff for publishing and media companies. This is the best way to get in at a low-level entry. You gain an insight into the company, can make contacts, find out about jobs coming up in the company before they are advertised, and, once you decide to move on, get your first job reference from within the industry. Gaining experience this way does not just inform you about the industry, it also gives a good impression of your commitment.

Speculative applications can provide a good source for employers looking for people for entry-level or junior posts. However, these have to be researched and presented particularly well.

Applying for a job in publishing

Have a good CV and covering letter. As a graduate you may have little professional experience, so concentrate on selling the transferable skills you have gained throughout your studies, for example, typing, languages, IT skills, numeracy and relevant experiences gained by, for instance, working on a campus magazine, setting up a website, voluntary work and so on.

The top requirement of an employer in the publishing industry is that a job applicant must be informed: that is, informed about the business generally, and specifically, the company they are seeking employment from. You should have no problem finding out about publishing houses and their products. One employer said that it was alarming how few people made the effort of going to a bookstore to look at the publisher's books on sale. You should also look at their catalogue, whether you order a printed version or look at it online. You will probably be asked for an opinion on their products, so think of something to say, such as how they differ from similar products from competitors, or how they were displayed in the store, or how good the design is and so on. As you are probably applying for a low-level job in the hierarchy, try not to lecture them on their own product. The main point is that you come across informed and interested. Before going for an interview, read the job advert you are applying for very carefully and check that you can match most of their requirements.

Never forget that publishing is a business aiming to be profitable. Whatever department you work in, you always need to be financially aware. At interview, candidates can disqualify themselves from the start by focussing on personal job fulfilment. For a company, your happiness is only in aid of making you work more efficiently for them.

You may be interviewed by your immediate boss, by somebody from personnel and/or by your boss's boss. Part of your interview may be a test: for editorial jobs you could be asked to proofread and edit on paper or within a desktop publishing program such as QuarkXpress. For production jobs you may be asked to prove your basic technical skills and do a paper calculation.

Be prepared to ask questions at the end of an interview. This is both your chance to find out more the job and company you are applying for, and, often more importantly for the interviewer, to enable them to gauge your interest. A first interview is not the place to discuss pay or working conditions. This can be discussed at a second interview or once you have been offered the job. Don't take rejection to heart. Sometimes interviews go really well and sometimes really badly, regardless of your qualifications. It can all be down to pure personal chemistry between you and the interviewer.

Case study: Alison Kennedy

Alison Kennedy is the Production and Distribution Director for Egmont UK, a large children's books publisher. Her career is a good example of how, with the right dedication and ability, you can move from a humble first-time job to directorial level. In her 32-year career in print and publishing, Alison has worked her way up from a shorthand typist to production director of a £26-million turnover children's publisher.

What does a publisher want from a first-job employee?

'We look for good attitude, enthusiasm, open-mindedness and a realisation that you have to start at the bottom even if you are hugely qualified. The qualities we look for in candidates are being positive, open-minded, enthusiastic and being prepared to be part of a team. Skills are less important in a first-time jobber. Attitude is with you for life, skills can be taught.'

What do you look for in a CV?

'A CV is vital. It should be short and to the point. It should be well laid out and not have any spelling or grammatical errors, which are a complete turn-off. It should also be presented in a professional rather than fun way.'

What does a job applicant need to do to have a successful job interview?

'Do some preparation before the interview and try to find out about the company and their aims. Always be well presented in your clothes, hair and so on. Most people make judgements within the first five minutes. Be interested and interesting. Get the balance right of finding out about the position, showing interest, but not to the detriment of being interesting about your own qualities.'

How competitive is the publishing industry?

'It is competitive to get into because it appears from the outside to be a very nice place to work. However, it is always a commercial situation and it has the same hard economic boundaries that any other industry has,

(Continued)

(Continued)

and this can be a little surprising for those that see it as a 'tea and bis-cuits' cottage industry.'

What technical skills are needed?

'We all expect keyboard skills nowadays. I would expect some knowledge of Word and something along the lines of Outlook, but I would not be put off by having to arrange training for the right person.'

Once in the job, how can the first-time employee advance?

'By being brilliant in their own field, but also by being inquisitive in how the whole publishing machine works, how everything fits together and information flows throughout the organisation. People who have the broadest view progress quickest and furthest.'

What advice would you offer to aspiring job seekers in your field in publishing?

- Seek (unpaid if you have to) work experience. Be prepared to see this as a key part of the investment in getting a job. If you have just invested three or four years in a degree, then a few weeks of unpaid work is a small additional investment.
- Be prepared to start at the bottom or even in another department. Getting your feet in the door and getting noticed is key.
- Show enthusiasm, even if the task is simply stuffing envelopes. Come up with an idea that saves money or makes the task quicker, or takes up less room.
- Be noticed for the right professional reasons.
- Network, network, network – this industry is all about who you know.
- Read business books, show you are interested beyond the basics and that you are open-minded to new ideas.

To summarise, employers in publishing look for graduates who are flexible, willing and enthusiastic. They are looking for bright people. Despite this, you may start off with very dull and mind-numbing paperwork and administrative jobs. Work hard and, while not neglecting your duties, be willing to do more than your job remit requires.

Publishers look for experience and relevant skills. The less training you need, the faster you can start working effectively. On the other hand, if you make a favourable impression in your interview and seem willing and able to gain the relevant experience fast, an employer may find it worth investing in you by supplying some basic on-the-job training.

In general, publishing jobs appeal to humanities students. However, science students are often preferred in editorial positions in many STM and specialist academic publishers because of their special subject knowledge. No single subject area is more favoured than another when it comes to filling general posts, because the bigger publishers cover such a vast array of subjects.

Resources

Useful books

Clark, G. (2001) *Inside Book Publishing: A Career Builder's Guide*. London: Routledge.
Harris, N. (1991) *Basic Editing: A Practical Course*, Vol. 1 The Text and Vol. 2 The Exercises. Wordsworth: Publishing Training Centre.
Butcher, J. (2006) *Butcher's Copy-Editing*. Cambridge: Cambridge University Press.
Baverstock, A. (2000) *How to Market Books*. London: Kogan Page.
Peacock, J. (1995) *Book Production*. London: Blueprint/Routledge.
Woll, T. (1999) *Publishing for Profit*. London: Kogan Page.

Useful websites

www.thebookseller.com – This website is based on *The Bookseller*, the weekly publication (published on Fridays) for the UK book publishing industry. A must to find out about recent news in the industry and to look at the jobs pages.

http://media.guardian.co.uk – The place to look for job advertisements. www.train4publishing.co.uk – The Publishing Training Centre (PTC) offers industry-recognised courses in most aspects of publishing, for the novice to refreshers. These courses are not cheap. It is worth looking at their links and their lists of college courses as well as their online guide to jobs in publishing.

www.workinpublishing.org.uk – Has a lot of useful background information about the publishing industry. It has good links to publishing courses and employment websites.

www.thesyp.org.uk/ – The Society of Young Publishers (SYP) is set up to help young professionals (18–35 years old) in the publishing industry, in particular book publishing. It is based in London and has a branch in Oxford. It is a place to socialise, network and learn from others in a similar junior situation.

FOURTEEN   Media librarianship

This chapter is written by Adrian Figgess, who was responsible for the libraries and archives at Granada Media between 1990 and 2002, oversee-ing the growth of the department as the company merged with other ITV companies. Prior to this, he was the Product Development Manager at BBC Enterprises Library Sales and more recently worked at the National Film and Television Archive as the Head of Conservation and Logistics.

Overview of media librarianship

Libraries and archives have been at the heart of media organisations for many years. They are a source of information, making books, journals, film, tape and written records available and providing safe and secure storage of the collections. Whilst digitisation is changing the way libraries operate and provide their services, the need for them remains. Whether storing physical items on shelves and retrieving them for bor-rowers or accessing information from computerised databases, the library continues to fulfil a vital function in many media organisations. It is a career that graduates with an interest in film and media may not have considered because it is less well-known that other occupations in the field.

What is a media library?

Most media organisations need a library of some kind. They vary in size from small collections of reference books or a shelf of cassettes to huge warehouses full of videotape and film cans. A formal media library comprises a managed, indexed collection of film, videotape, audio tape, written records, books/journals, photographs – or a combi-nation of these. Increasingly, the digital age means that we can add the computer file to this list: more and more television and radio pro-grammes are being stored in this way, as are written records, newspa-pers and photographs. There is no longer necessarily a difference in meaning between the terms 'library' and 'archive'. The terms have become largely interchangeable, with the word 'archive' becoming more contemporary with the advent of digital technology and the consequent ability to store things 'indefinitely' as computer files.

The following are examples of the libraries that might be found in a television company:

- film library
- tape library
- reference library
- stills library
- written records archive.

Now that so much information is available, online resources are no longer used as intensively as researchers can do much of their initial work at their desk. Some material used in television programmes and films is bought in from external collections and some libraries sell content to others.

What do media librarians do?

Librarians have a range of functions, some of which are listed below; television has one of the most diverse ranges of library work, so we have used television libraries as an example:

- Supply of blank tape to a technical area, studio or cameraman.
- Supply of existing tapes to be used in editing or for dubbing (copying).
- Supply of existing tapes for playout (including broadcast).
- Shipping tapes to another broadcaster.
- Answering general enquiries concerning tape and its content.
- Compiling required sections of recordings on to a single tape.
- Digitisation (ingest of content from tape on to a server).
- Wiping/recycling used tape.
- Intake of blank tape stock from a commercial supplier.
- Add the output of the press office (photographs taken to promote an actor/programme) into the collection.
- Select stills to be used in the press pack when programmes are marketed.
- Manage the digital ingestion of selected stills into the library.
- Generate copies of stills as required.
- Provide a research/access facility for customers.
- Obtain stills from external agencies for use in a programme.
- Provide advice and help regarding information sources.
- Maintain the stock of books, journals and other publications.
- Borrow (purchase) books from external libraries (suppliers).
- Manage the subscriptions to online resources.
- Carry out research on behalf of customers.

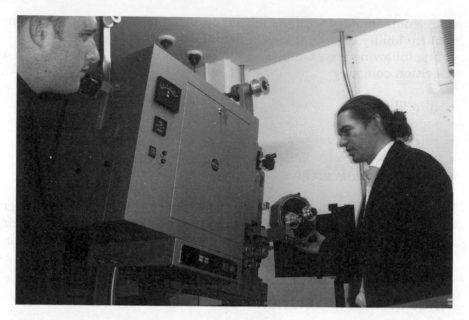

Understanding how to handle film stock is vital

In general, the main role of the librarian is to access the holdings of the various collections and make them (or information about them) available to the client. Overall management of the collections, including housekeeping and maintenance, must be carried out, with removal of items according to strict rules. Wiping the wrong tape can be disastrous – and expensive!

What background and skills do media librarians need?

Media librarians come from a wide variety of backgrounds:

- directly from college/university, perhaps with a media studies qualification which can be helpful in providing context
- a library in another sector
- outside the media sector (but ideally with an appreciation of, or experience in, a related sector like theatre, publishing or electronics).

Skills required by librarians include:

- in television, a basic understanding of the production, editing and playout processes
- customer service skills

- organisational skills
- general computer skills (MS Windows, Office and so on).

Personal characteristics include:

- good attention to detail
- interest in the particular media sector (TV, radio, film, newspapers and so on)
- ability to work to deadlines
- high standards of literacy and numeracy
- a sense of order
- a desire to work with people and provide a good service
- a willingness to be flexible.

Where could a graduate find media librarian jobs?

Opportunities for the work exist in all media sectors; television, radio, newspapers and photographic agencies. All have libraries of some sort or other – and therefore need librarians to run them. However, the role of a librarian can vary greatly from one organisation to another – and it continues to change.

Where are media library jobs located?

In the UK, the main collections are generated by the major media organisations, such as in film: Pathé Distribution, Warner Brothers and UIP; in television: Sky Television, the BBC and other big players like ITV, Channel 4 and RTL (owners of TV channel 'Five'); in newspapers and magazines: News International, Trinity Mirror Group and Emap. There are also the publicly funded film and television archives: the National Film and Television Archive (administered by the British Film Institute), plus archives in each of Scotland, Wales, Northern Ireland and the Irish Republic, together with several regional collections. In addition, there are the National Museum of Film, Photography and Television and the National Sound Archive. A useful list of archives is provided on the 'Moving History' website.

Most of the principal media organisations have their headquarters in London, but there are significant media 'clusters' in other cities around Britain, such as Manchester, Leeds and Glasgow. In addition, there are many smaller companies operating throughout the country, although many of these will not have their collections constituted as formal 'libraries'.

Internationally, many major cities have a television, radio and newspaper presence – and some have film production activity.

Some universities and colleges running media studies courses will have links with media organisations. Take advantage of these to obtain placements, vacation work and so on. Once 'inside', you can get to know people who will be valuable contacts when you are seeking your first position. This is important because not all media librarian jobs are advertised – you are more likely to see vacancies for camera people, editors, journalists, producers and so forth. It may thus be advisable to gain employment of some other kind with the chosen organisation and seek to transfer to the library once there.

A list of the main employers is given at the end of this chapter, along with other useful contact details.

What is the salary like?

Except for the most senior positions, librarians are not generally highly paid, and the media sector is no exception. However, salaries are comparable with other media roles and librarianship offers the prospect of developing transferable skills which will be useful not only elsewhere in the organisation, but also in almost any career path for those choosing not to stay working in the media.

What progress or promotion is Possible?

The larger libraries have more varied work, more staff and therefore more opportunities to progress and learn different aspects of media librarianship. A good career path would involve working in several (or all) of them. If your prospective employer doesn't offer this, it is worth asking for it: such a proactive approach on your part should be well received and may prompt the development of a structured career path for librarians in the organisation.

What is the future for media libraries?

All types of libraries have been affected by the huge technological advances brought about by the computer. Access to vast amounts of information and data is now possible from one's desk, rendering some traditional library services obsolete. A television programme, still photograph, rehearsal script and last week's newspaper can all now be stored – and accessed – as digital files.

However, as has been stated above, the specialised knowledge of a librarian is not all available on a PC and as yet, not everything has been digitised – perhaps some material never will be, given the potential costs (including the implications for cataloguing) that that implies. Consequently, a career as a media librarian is still viable, although you should be prepared for a role that will change a great deal along the way.

The librarian of the future may spend more time guiding the customer through what is becoming an apparently infinite amount of information available over the web as the latter may know (roughly?) what he/she requires but may not be very efficient in finding it.

Information specialists could work directly with authors, advertising agencies, journalists, TV programme-makers and so on to advise on appropriate information sources and how to find them, whilst a training role could be developed in order to pass on searching techniques and other knowledge to users.

Libraries will become increasingly concerned with content rather than carrier, building up centralised information resources and basic techniques that individuals will not find cost-effective to develop themselves. For example, in the fields of film and television, areas such as rights management, simple editing (that is, adjusting programme breaks in television shows) and copying between formats may become library functions as the advantages of centralising content management become apparent.

There will thus be plenty of physical film, tape, books, stills and journals to be stored and accessed for many years yet, so the need for their management will persist. However, it is not unreasonable to think that, in these cost-cutting times, management of some aspects of media library work might be outsourced; an example might be the routine tasks of physical materials handling thereby separating the management of content and carrier.

The future structure of the small screen media industry is likely to be configured as separate components: the large-scale producer – broadcasters such as the BBC and ITV with their own in-house library functions and other facilities will give way to smaller, more focused organisations each trading with the other in a fashion comparable to that in which the independent production and facilities sectors already operate. Thus it is not difficult to envisage a Media Libraries Ltd providing all the various library services to anyone who wants them. Subject to issues of confidentiality and security, therefore, Channel 4's written archives could be stored by the same organisation managing the BBC stills collection and ITV's tapes. This could be a highly cost-effective business model that would see media owners cooperating to their mutual benefit.

Case study: Dave

Dave is a television librarian in ITV with many years' experience. We asked him about his job.

Can you describe what you do?

'I currently work in the stills library at ITV Granada in Manchester, mainly with the photographs used by the Press Office to publicise the programmes. The primary role of the stills librarian is to archive these digital still images on to a server after the programme has been transmitted.'

'We currently use Cumulus 6.5 software to manage the images: this is a digital asset management system which enables us to make a large selection of stills available to various user departments throughout ITV.'

'Another task is accessing the hard copy back catalogue, scanning and captioning older images as required. As not all new stills are taken using a digital camera, there is a continuing need to accession contact sheets and negatives into the library.'

'We work on a supply-and-demand basis to newspapers, magazines, television programmes, books and so on, both internally within ITV and externally, generating an income for ITV Library Services. Images are generally sent out by e-mail. Over the years, I have worked in most sections of Library Services, including the VT (tape) Library, the News Library and International Despatch; I have also covered for colleagues in other areas.'

How did you get into it? Was it what you planned or did you happen upon it?

'I was interested in working in television but had a job as a purchase ledger clerk – which is a totally different environment. However, my father worked at Granada and I went along to observe how the library worked. Later, I applied when a vacancy came up in the VT Library, and got the job.'

What training did you receive?

'Within the stills library, I received specific training for the Cumulus software plus on-the-job training from a colleague. You learn a lot just by doing the job: having worked in several different areas of the library, I have built up a significant amount of knowledge, for example, new computer skills. I did not know much about photography before becoming the stills librarian.'

What are the key skills in your job role?

'It is important to have a good general knowledge of Granada's programmes and, ideally, those originating from the other parts of ITV, as we

(Continued)

receive queries about all of them. Having the inclination to protect and preserve the collection is important as well, with a sense of order (so understanding captioning and indexing is key too). A passion for archiving helps, particularly as much of what is kept is only requested occasionally, so you have to be self-motivated and feel quite driven in the work.'

'Other characteristics you need include being well-organised, having a good telephone manner, good communication skills and being approachable from the customer's perspective. Oh, and being passionate about television is useful.'

What technical skills are important?

'These are mainly computer-based skills: on a daily basis, I use the Cumulus software with the Imation Disk Stacker and the Nikon Super Cool 9000 scanner, along with standard software like Outlook, Word, Internet Explorer and Adobe Photoshop.'

Highs and lows – what are the most satisfying aspects of the work? What are the least?

'It is very satisfying to be able to supply stills on demand, often with a tight deadline: images can sometimes be needed by a programme within 30 minutes of going on air. I take great pleasure in working with and maintaining one of the best stills archives in the UK (in my opinion!), knowing that the images are correctly captioned, catalogued and stored.'

'On the downside, the ability to capture images more cheaply brought about by digital technology has caused many more to be taken, resulting in difficult decisions regarding what should be kept and what deleted. The server is not large enough to accommodate everything, and captioning such a large volume would be very time-consuming and not cost-effective. We thus have a large backlog, which can be frustrating.'

What advice would you offer to aspiring media librarians?

'To be prepared to start at the bottom. In all the library areas, you learn on the job, so starting at the beginning is sensible. I've always had specific training if I needed it, but there is no substitute for actually doing the job alongside colleagues. You do need to be driven – offering to spend holidays working whilst still a student (for nothing if necessary) provides valuable experience, for example – and it is a useful stepping stone to other roles in television because of the contacts made through the library.

How do people get jobs in media libraries?

'The best way is to obtain work experience and/or vacation work; try to meet with the manager of the department you want to work in; ask to be shown around – generally, get your face known!'

(Continued)

(Continued)

'Obviously, you will have to apply for the relevant job eventually, but it certainly helps if you have been doing it on an informal basis already!'

What do you see as the future of this work?

'As much of library work is now computerised, the main changes are going to be technology-based, in particular the digitisation and centralisation of our holdings across ITV – virtually, if not physically, making access easier for librarians and staff in general. Local knowledge about programmes and production will continue to be important though, I think.'

What about your own future? What are your ambitions?

'I would like to work more closely alongside my Picture Desk colleagues in the Press Office, observing their role and possibly bringing the two roles together in some way. I would also like to be involved in the management and integration of the stills libraries across ITV as a whole: I can see where this would help with some of our problems and it would be very satisfying being able to implement some of the solutions.'

Useful addresses

UK radio broadcasters

BBC
The BBC provides national and local radio services throughout the UK. It also provides the World Service, funded by the Foreign Office.

BBC Recruitment
PO Box 48305
London
W12 6YE
E-mail: recruitment@bbc.co.uk
web: www.bbc.co.uk/jobs/ is the BBC Jobs home page which gives a great deal of information about how to join the Corporation. The BBC also holds careers fairs.

Oneword Radio
UBC Media Group plc
50 Lisson Street
London
NW1 5DF
Tel: 0207 453 1600
Fax: 0207 723 6132
E-mail: info1@ubcmedia.com
web: www.oneword.co.uk/

Channel Four Radio
Channel 4 Television
124 Horseferry Road
London SW1P 2TX
Tel: 0207 396 4444
web: www.channel4radio.com/

Talk Sport
talkSPORT
18 Hatfields
London
SE1 8DJ
Tel: 08704 202020
web: www2.talksport.net/jobs/jobs.asp

RTÉ
RTÉ
Donnybrook
Dublin 4
Tel: 00 353 1 208 3111
Fax: 00 353 1 208 3080
web: www.rte.ie/
E-mail: info@rte.ie
web: www.rte.ie/laweb/index.html RTÉ have a specific site for their
Libraries and Archives department
The BBC in Scotland, Wales and Northern Ireland also produces and
broadcasts programmes in Gaelic, Welsh and Irish respectively. RTÉ,
the national state broadcaster for the Republic of Ireland, has dedicated
Irish-language radio and television stations.

UK television broadcasters

BBC
The BBC has many television channels and interests in several
others. It provides local news and a small amount of regional
programming.

BBC Recruitment
PO Box 48305
London
W12 6YE
E-mail: recruitment@bbc.co.uk
web: www.bbc.co.uk/jobs/ is the BBC jobs home page which gives a
great deal of information about how to join the Corporation. The BBC
also holds careers fairs.

ITV

ITV currently has five television channels. Its main business is nationally networked television, but it also provides local news and a small amount of regional programming. Contact is via the individual ITV sites, but in the first instance visit www.iTVjobs.com/. This site has case studies of people who have had careers in ITV and plenty of help about submitting CVs and work experience at the individual ITV sites.

Channel 4

Channel 4 Television
124 Horseferry Road
London SW1P 2TX
Tel: 0207 396 4444

Channel Four has several channels currently on air, including a dedicated film channel, FilmFour. Information about working there is contained at www.channel4.com/4careers/4careers_new/. There is also a section of the website aimed at Media Studies students: www.channel4.com/learning/microsites/W/wtc4/.

Five

Five
22 Long Acre
London
WC2E 9LY
Tel: 08457 050505
Fax: 0207 421 7270
E-mail: customerservices@five.TV
web: www.five.TV/aboutfive/recruitment/

Sky

Sky provides a large number of television channels as well as distributing many others via its UK subscriber system. Sky News also provides a news service for radio stations.

British Sky Broadcasting Group
Grant Way
Isleworth
TW7 5QD
Tel: 0207 705 3000
E-mail: queries@bskyb.com
web: jobs.sky.com/

International broadcasters

Some of the principal public broadcasters in the English-speaking world include:

Australia (ABC) – www.abc.net.au/
Canada (CBC) – www.cbc.ca/
New Zealand (TVNZ) – http://tvnz.co.nz/
South Africa (SABC) – www.sabc.co.za/
United States (PBS) – www.pbs.org/

In addition, organisations in non-English-speaking countries often produce material in English for international broadcast. Here are a few examples:

Sweden (Radio Sweden) – www.sr.se/rs/english/
Czech Republic (Radio Prague) – www.radio.cz/english/
China (China Radio International) – http://en.chinabroadcast.cn/
Japan (NHK) – www.nhk.or.jp/english/
Germany (Deutsche Welle) – www.dw-world.de/
France (RFI) – www.rfi.fr/langues/statiques/rfi_anglais.asp

Press

British Newspapers and News Online
Links to all the national, regional and local newspapers throughout Britain and Ireland that publish online news and information. All the major titles are covered.
web: www.wrx.zen.co.uk/britnews.htm.

Press Association Archive
web: www.eastriding.gov.uk/libraries/libraries/pressarchive.html

Press Association Cuttings Library
The Press Association's main text library contains 14 million cuttings, with a range of national and regional newspaper content, as well as a selection of key magazines.
Tel: 0870 830 6824.
E-mail: newslibrary@pa.press.net
web: www.palibrary.press.net

Stills

The online Film and Video Directory's list of stills libraries.
web: www.4rfv.co.uk/fulllisting.asp?scategory=275

BAPLA

BAPLA is the UK trade association for picture libraries and the largest organisation of its kind in the world. With over 400 member companies, it represents the vast majority of commercial picture libraries and agencies in the UK.
web: www.bapla.org.uk/static/bapla/

Other useful links

Moving History is a research guide to the United Kingdom's twelve public sector film archives but also has a large list of other resources, archives and related organisations.
web: www.movinghistory.ac.uk/links/index.html

ITN Source is a major provider of broadcast content, with more than 700,000 hours of footage. It represents several collections, including those of Reuters, Granada, Channel 4, Fox and British Pathe.
web: www.itnsource.com/About_Us/

The BBC equivalent to ITN Source is the **BBC Motion Gallery**.
web: www.bbcmotiongallery.com/

The Film Archive Forum website has links to all the UK national and regional archives and the Imperial War Museum Film and Video Archive.
web: www.bufvc.ac.uk/faf/faf.htm

The online **Film and Video Directory** has listings of film laboratories and storage companies, archives, music libraries, record companies and stills libraries.
web: www.4rfv.co.uk/directory.asp

FOCAL International (The Federation of Commercial Audiovisual Libraries) is a membership-based organisation concerned with clips/extracts/stock footage. Members include libraries, consultants and researchers.
web: www.focalint.org/index.htm

AUKML (The Association of UK Media Librarians) is an organisation for print and broadcast news librarians, news researchers and information workers in the media industry. Members come from newspaper and magazine publishing, broadcasting organisations and academic institutions.
AUKML
PO Box 14254
London
SE1 9WL
E-mail: membership@aukml.org.uk
web: www.aukml.org.uk/

FIFTEEN   Multimedia

It hardly needs stating that technology has transformed every aspect of our life in the last decades. The beginning of the transformation can be traced to the launch of Microsoft in 1975. Bill Gates recognised the potential of technology to extend the power of computers to individuals. Computers ceased to be the stereotypical, difficult, scientific machines that only men in white lab coats could possibly understand or operate. They evolved into everyday objects that most people could master. Children use them as toys; adults use them for work, entertainment and leisure. They are in most of our homes and are the tools we completely rely upon to run our financial and commercial world. In the arts too, technology has opened up new and exciting realms to challenge human creative instincts. Their use in the production of film, music, broadcasting and journalism is so extensive that it is difficult to imagine how these industries ever operated without computing technologies.

As they have developed, so computer technologies have created an incredible range of opportunities for work. Researchers write that of the children currently in primary school, 20 per cent will have a job that doesn't even exist yet.

What is multimedia exactly? Multimedia is typically thought of as CD-ROMs, DVDs, websites and video installations containing images, text, sound, animation, graphics and so on.

What do multimedia designers do? Multimedia designers (sometimes called multimedia developers) plan, manage, design and author these productions, usually to a client brief. Producing multimedia can involve detailed negotiations and communications with clients and customers to ensure that what is produced meets their requirements. Specialist roles within multimedia include graphic design, illustration, animation, digital film and sound. Once the product has been developed, it usually requires exhaustive testing to ensure that it works as it should, and that the client is fully satisfied with the product.

Skills in multimedia

This is essentially a technical, computing role. There are several specialisms within multimedia, but typical skills requirements are a level of expertise in the industry standard software programs including authorware Macromedia Director, Macromedia Flash, Dreamweaver and Photoshop. These are highly complex and evolving programs, with new variants frequently being launched, so a real enthusiasm for, and ability with, computing is absolutely vital. Multimedia designers should be able to work effectively as a member of a team because the work requires a highly structured team approach. However, they must also be able to concentrate on solitary, individual work whilst programming or designing. Multimedia developers must communicate clearly and precisely in speech and writing, have an eye for detail and be well organised. It is obvious that creativity and enthusiasm for the work are vital.

Career opportunities

Because CIT (communications and information technology) is such a huge field, there are many potential employers for multimedia designers. Education, health, retail, advertising and marketing, software companies, computer manufacturers and many small, medium-sized and large organisations may employ multimedia designers, as the following vacancies indicate. With experience, you can become self-employed or freelance.

As with many CIT professions, there seem to be more opportunities in the southeast of England, London and the major regional cities. But because multimedia is so varied, and there are many smaller companies and universities employing multimedia developers, it should be possible to find openings in most parts of the UK.

Salaries for multimedia developers relate well to average graduate-level salaries for other types of CIT work. With experience, and particularly if self-employment is an option, they can be well above average.

What progress or promotion is possible?

Because the skills involved in multimedia are perfectly transferable between employers, it is fairly straightforward to move companies in order to get more responsibility, more money and a better job. As with many graduate and technical jobs, the next stage up is very often into management, so multimedia designers, as their career progresses, may well find themselves doing a lot less on the computer screen and a lot more interaction with staff, colleagues and clients.

Case study: Kevan Williams

Kevan Williams is a multimedia designer in a university Learning Development Unit.

Can you describe what you do?

'I am a multimedia development officer in a Learning Development Unit in a large university. We develop electronic learning materials and at the moment I am working with Macromedia Breeze, a webconferencing technology. I work closely with academic staff in order to understand how they currently teach, and finding ways to translate that knowledge into effective online products. It involves explaining and demonstrating to academics how technologies can be used to enhance what they do – not to replace them, but to make their teaching better. I use audio, video and graphics to show academics how technology can make their teaching more effective.'

How did you get into it? Was it what you planned or did you happen upon it?

'I was actually a Public Relations student looking to break into a more technical role. I knew I didn't want to go into PR but I'd always been interested in technology and computers, right from being a kid. I had to undertake a project and the one I chose involved researching the text content of a CD-ROM about PR. I completed the project and was immediately offered three months' paid work to develop the CD-ROM further. Once that was completed, I was invited to do the same thing again for another production – this one was about psychology, which I knew nothing about. I proved my ability in that first 12-month period, working as a 'User Documentation Development Officer', I was willing and tried to solve problems myself rather than pester other staff. Basically, I made myself irreplaceable!'

What training did you receive? Do you get more training now?

'I got three days' Authorware training in Nottingham once! To be honest, all the training has been on-the-job. I was mentored by experienced staff when I first arrived, but as they left I became senior, and now I am the most experienced person in my area here. When I have to learn a new program or get familiar with updates to programs, I just work at it until I master it. I read up on my field and keep up with new developments – you have to because this work changes rapidly and continually.'

(Continued)

(Continued)

What are the key skills in your job role?

'The most important from the start is communication. I have to be able to liaise with everybody in the institution from the technicians to the Vice Chancellor. I have to give presentations to a wide range of audiences about what we do in the unit. I have to be able to interpret technology and translate in a clear way to people who have little understanding of my subject. I must communicate effectively with my project team and present CD-ROMs to clients.

'Aside from communication, personality is very important. I am not a stereotype techno-geek; I'm more of a front man (it helps that I've worked behind a bar for 14 years!).

'I'd also say you need to be someone who can really apply themselves to a problem and be able to get on with a task once you're given it. There are always problems with technology and you should not give up until you've truly exhausted all the possibilities and you are sure you can't solve it yourself. Don't be running to someone asking questions because you'll be more of a hindrance than a help.'

What technical skills are important?

'I use on a regular, daily basis a wide range of technical programs, such as:

- Macromedia Authorware
- Macromedia Flash
- Macromedia Breeze
- Adobe Photoshop
- Adobe Premier
- Helix Producer
- Windows Media Encoder
- The Office Suite.

And lots of subsidiary products.'

Highs and lows – what are the most satisfying aspects of the work? What are the worst?

'The best things about this job are the respect I get from colleagues outside the institution, being valued for my expertise and knowledge and the feeling that I am a positive influence in the organisation. I have a lot of flexibility and autonomy. It's also rewarding to develop something, then seeing clients using and enjoying it.

'The drawbacks are not having my own budget – sometimes I know I need a certain piece of kit and I have to battle to get the finance for it, which holds up the work unnecessarily. I get fed up with people's inability to appreciate how long it takes to do what I do – the over-expectation of clients

(Continued)

that a CD-ROM will do everything for them and replace their teaching. It doesn't always have the impact they expect. It is annoying when people with no technical understanding refer to me as a 'technician' – they just don't understand what you do.'

What advice would you offer to aspiring multimedia designers?

'You can't be a jack of all trades. Learn to do something and do it well. For instance, when I employ someone to do some video work, I want them to be able to do *all* the video work that comes in; to be expert. You've got to choose what you're going to be and master it.'

What are the key skills for success? How could a person with a film or media degree best approach entry into the career?

'You could get what you need from your degree, depending on what is covered in modules, but work experience is critical. Get work experience either within your degree or outside it. Keep in contact with people you meet on work experience because they will be links to other opportunities. For instance, if other companies phone me looking for someone I'll remember someone from work experience and if they were good, recommend them. If you are stuck, phone people in multimedia and ask for advice. The advice I'd give would change on a monthly basis – because the job changes that quickly.'

How do people get jobs in multimedia?

'If we are looking for someone here for a vacancy, I'll ask around to see if anyone knows someone looking for a job, because the ones who've made the effort to be in contact will be in people's minds. It's the proactive ones who stand out from the crowd who get the jobs; the ones who do something that makes you remember them.'

'There are advertised vacancies, particularly on the web, but the ones I know who have got jobs have made that initial contact.'

What do you see as the future of this work?

'As educational institutions move into the global market, there is no doubt in my mind that there will be an explosion of need for multimedia developers. The web is growing at such a rate yet there are still companies that don't believe they need a website! There is a big gap and a huge need for people who can develop content. It's constantly growing.'

What about your own future? What are your ambitions?

'My ideal role would be a Systems Integration Officer. This would be a more strategic approach to implementing the technologies across the institution. I can see where such a role would solve a lot of organisational problems, and I get frustrated now by seeing things that could be better and not being able to implement them.'

Multimedia in education and training

There is an increasing use of technology in schools, colleges and universities and this is likely to increase still further. Multimedia is just one aspect of IT in education, and there is a huge investment to be made in training, facilities and equipment. However, prospects look bright for a graduate with an interest in media and IT to combine visual and technical skills within an educational development department. With increasing interest in distance learning, open learning and e-learning, this area is likely to offer exciting new career prospects in the future.

In addition to conventional educational contexts such as colleges, there are jobs in e-training and development for private and business clients. The process is similar in both fields: to understand your clients' needs and to develop engaging and useable solutions to help them deliver the information they want.

Multimedia publishing

A huge and fast-growing career area within multimedia is publishing. Of course, printing books and magazines onto paper will remain an option, but increasingly news, entertainment and communications are being prepared and broadcast entirely digitally. The work has many aspects, from writing and photography to sales and business development. Work could involve creating regional web pages, news websites, sports pages, customising information to individual needs and many other exciting developments. The meeting between the conventional, traditional worlds of journalism, writing and filming with the digital world is often referred to as 'convergence'. This convergence is likely to grow as, for example, people are beginning to publish e-books just on the web and these innovations are likely to increase, with a concurrent increase in jobs.

Multimedia games designer

One of the areas most likely to appeal to creative types who are also IT competent is games designing. Games are a vast billion-pound and increasing market, potentially far outstripping films. There are now many courses specialising in games design, including postgraduate ones if you have a relevant first degree or good experience. Again, this is an area which changes very quickly, so seek expert advice for current information.

Career suggestions for multimedia

If you wish to pursue this career or find out more, here are some ideas.

Find out if your university has a department which develops multimedia. It may have different names, so ask in the library if you're not sure. If you have left university you could contact the institution nearest your home or try local colleges. Get in contact either in person, by telephone or by email, and try to arrange a visit to talk to a multimedia designer or developer (again they might be called something different). See if you can organise some short work experience for yourself to see if you are really right for the job.

If you are technically competent, teach yourself one or more of the key programs mentioned above. Many web developers are self-taught, but you should only attempt this if you have access to a good PC and have a flair for technology. otherwise you may become very frustrated.

If you cannot access suitable training in your current role, you may be able to do a short course at a local college, night school, a private organisation or online. Check on the Internet for up-to-date information as this field changes very rapidly.

Resources

www.bima.co.uk – The British Interactive Media Association website.

Index

acting (actor), 125, 130–1, 137
AGCAS, *see* Association of Graduate
    Careers Advisory Services (AGCAS)
AHRC, *see* Arts and Humanities Research
    Board, the (AHRC)
airtime sales, 151
animation, 21, 125, 136
application(s), 3, 5, 43, 54, 66–7, 70, 72,
    77–118, 191
APTN, *see* Associated Press Television
    News (APTN)
Ariel, 141
art director, 132
Arts and Humanities Research Board,
    the (AHRC), 11
assertiveness, 3, 60–5, 67
Associated Press Television News
    (APTN), 144
Association of Graduate Careers Advisory
    Services (AGCAS), 8, 25
audio-visual industries, 7–8, 11, 15, 19, 21,
    24–5, 29, 32, 38, 127

BAFTA, 141
BBC, 13, 15, 53, 132, 135, 138–41,
    144–5, 147, 149–50, 154–5, 160–1,
    196, 199, 201
BFI, *see* British Film Institute (BFI)
body language, 59, 63
Bollywood, 125
Bookseller, 191
British Film Institute (BFI), 145, 199
Broadcast, 141
broadcasting, 1, 7, 11, 20, 24–5, 29, 32,
    126, 135–45, 147–54, 197, 201, 209
Broadcasting Act, 14

cable and satellite television, 25, 135
CAD, *see* computer-aided design (CAD)
camera operator/cameraman, 130, 137,
    139, 142
camera skills, 144
camera work, 125
career fairs, 56, 142

Channel 4, 67, 135, 140–1, 143,
    199, 201
charities, 11, 19, 34, 36, 45
Chicken Tikka Masala, 127
CIT, *see* communications and information
    technology (CIT)
CNN, 138–9, 144
communication skills, 13, 22, 26–7, 37,
    41, 44, 71, 117, 151, 156, 179, 203,
    210, 212
communications and information
    technology (CIT), 210
composer, 137
computer-aided design (CAD), 125
copywriter, 41
corporate media, 19
costume design, 125
Country Life, 172
covering letters, 97, 102
creative and cultural industries,
    25, 28–30, 130
curriculum vitae (CV), 37, 41–3, 55, 58, 77,
    79, 83, 87–90, 94, 97–105, 118, 128,
    155, 177–81, 192–3
CV, *see* curriculum vitae (CV)

dailies (type of employment), 125
Daily Mail, the, 161, 172
director of photography, 137
DJ, 149, 141
documentary, 135–7, 140–1, 145

Edinburgh Television Festival, 144
Empire, 172
employability,
    auditing, 40–51, 54, 7
    definition, 39–40
    employers' perspective, 3, 24, 26, 29
    enhancing, 51–4
    overview, 125
entrepreneurial skills, 56

factual programming, 136
FHM, 175

film industry, 2–3, 7–8, 11–12, 15–16,
    19–21, 23–5, 29–30, 34, 39, 76, 97–8,
    123, 125–34
  careers in,
    director, 39, 90, 125, 127, 129–30
    distributor, 125
    editor, 125, 127
    graphic, 125
    hairdresser, 125, 127
    lighting specialist, 125
    make-up artist, 125
    producer, 127, 132
Financial Times, the, 172
floor manager, 138
freelancing, 13, 24–5, 32–4, 40, 51–2,
    56, 67, 126, 132, 154, 174, 178, 186,
    188, 190–1

Glamour, 176
Granada, 145, 186, 202
Guardian, the, 129, 141–2, 160, 191

halo effect, 58
health and safety, 75
Heat, 175
HECSU, *see* Higher Education Careers
    Service Unit (HECSU)
Hello, 68
Higher Education Careers Service Unit
    (HECSU), 26
Hollywood, 125

Independent, the, 161, 165
International Visual Communication
    Association (IVCA), 19
interpersonal skills, 27, 31, 44, 70, 84, 156
interview(s), 3, 5, 12, 20, 27, 29, 31, 36,
    43–4, 47, 58, 64, 68, 70, 74, 77, 79,
    86, 97, 111–16, 118, 133, 138, 141–2,
    151–2, 154–6, 159, 163, 175, 179–80,
    186, 192–4
in-tray exercise, 117
ITV, 13, 132, 135, 143–5, 196, 199,
    201–2, 204
IVCA, *see* International Visual
    Communication Association (IVCA)

journalism, 2, 10, 12, 17, 76, 100, 123–4,
    129, 209

key skills, 26

labour market information, 3
leadership skills, 22, 26–7, 45, 77

librarianship, 22
locations assistant, 132

magazines, 68, 123, 163, 169–70,
    172–82, 184
  careers in,
    designer, 176–7
    editor, 172, 174, 177–8
    editorial assistant, 172
    journalist, 172–4, 179
    publisher, 172, 178
    reporter, 174, 178–9
    sub-editor, 172, 174–7, 179
    writer, 173–4, 177, 179
media librarianship, 196–208
  careers in, stills librarian, 202–4
multimedia, 123, 140, 209–15
  careers in,
    designer, 209–15
    developer, 210, 213, 215
    development officer, 211
    games designer, 214
    publisher, 214
    teacher/trainer, 214
museum and gallery work, 22, 52
music critic, 39

negotiation skills, 55–65, 76
networking, 3, 5, 55–66, 71–2, 78, 127,
    141, 172, 194
News of the World, the, 165
newspaper(s), 12, 15, 19, 73, 75, 123, 127,
    138, 142, 161–70, 172–3, 175–6, 184,
    191, 199–200
  careers in,
    editor, 163–4
    editorial assistant, 168
    journalist, 161–8
    page designer, 164
    reporter, 137–40, 162–7
    researcher, 168
    sub-editor, 164
    writer, 162–4, 169–70
New Street Law, 132

on-line applications, 79
oovs, *see* out of vision stories (oovs)
out of vision stories (oovs), 138–9

Pathé Distribution, 199
PDP, *see* personal development
    planning (PDP)
personal development planning (PDP),
    1, 124

post-production, 125
PR, *see* public relations (PR)
presentation(s), 44, 61, 71, 79, 97,
   109–11, 117
presentation skills, 22, 44
production assistant, 133
prop- and model-making, 125
psychometric testing, 117
public relations (PR), 10, 19–20, 176, 211
publishing, 2, 71, 123, 183–95, 198
   careers in,
      commissioning editor, 187
      copy-editor, 188, 190
      designer, 188
      editor, 187, 190–2
      editorial assistant, 187
      illustrator, 190
      licensing or rights department, 190
      manufacturing controller, 188
      marketing and publicity, 189
      picture researcher, 190
      production controller, 183–4, 188
      production director, 193
      production editor, 187, 190
      proofreader, 190
      reprint controller, 183
      sales representative, 189
      services department, 190

radio, 2–3, 8, 11–12, 14–21, 25, 52, 57, 69,
   82, 96, 98, 123, 138, 140, 147–60, 163,
   173, 173, 199–200
   careers in,
      director, 151, 153
      editor, 147, 151, 153
      journalist, 17, 148–50, 154–9
      presenter, 17, 149–50, 154–6
      producer, 147–8, 150–1, 155, 157
      programme controller, 151
      reporter, 147–8, 155, 157
      writer, 151, 157
recruitment strategies, 15
Reuters, 139, 144
RTL, 199
runner, 127–9, 138, 143

screenwriter, 127
script editor, 21
scriptwriter, 21
self-employment, 8, 24–6, 40, 51–2, 56, 67,
   132, 210
self-management, 22, 132
self-presentation, 55–65, 108

self-promotion, 55–65
set design, 125
shorthand, 165–8, 179
Skillset, 2, 8, 11, 14–15, 21, 25, 29–30,
   127, 147, 160
Sky, 135, 139–41, 144–5, 173, 176, 199
SMART goals, 90–4
soft skills, 26, 37
sound engineer, sound engineering,
   125, 137
speculative application(s), 77, 79, 96,
   105, 112, 192
storyboarder/storyboarding, 21, 96
Sunday Times, The, 67, 168, 173

teamwork, 2–8, 45, 52, 77, 85, 117,
   126, 210
television, 2–3, 7–8, 11–16, 19–21, 39, 57,
   67, 82, 96, 123, 135–47, 155, 163, 181,
   196–203
   careers in,
      channel controller, 142
      correspondent, 142
      director, 137
      editor, 138–9, 141–2, 201
      journalist, 138–44
      lighting director, 137
      news editor, 137, 139, 142–3
      producer, 142
      reporter, 140, 142–3
      researcher, 142
      writer, 137, 140
terrestrial channels, 135
time management, 22
Times, The, 161, 168
transferable skills, 22, 26, 69, 78, 192,
   200, 210

visual skills, 8
voluntary work, 10, 23, 31, 35, 43, 69–70,
   89, 192
VT editor, 137

Warner Brothers, 199
work experience, 3, 5, 10, 12, 15, 17–19,
   22–3, 29, 33, 36, 57, 63–4, 66–79, 81,
   84, 86, 89, 102–3, 107, 110, 114, 132–3,
   141, 151, 154–7, 163, 166–8, 170, 175,
   177–8, 191, 194, 203, 213, 215
work placement(s), 3, 22, 56, 63–5, 68, 78,
   142, 145, 152, 155–7, 166, 168, 172,
   178, 200
work shadowing, 67, 70, 157, 163, 178